To dea[r]
With [...] [memo]ries
of the race Track on
Leasowmonth!
Happy 60 years!
and many more to
follow --
all my love
Deb tx
March 2001

FERRARI

THE RACING CARS

KEITH BLUEMEL

SUTTON PUBLISHING

First published in the United Kingdom in 2000 by
Sutton Publishing Limited · Phoenix Mill · Thrupp · Stroud
Gloucestershire GL5 2BU

A catalogue record for this book is available from the British Library.

ISBN 0 7509 2487 X

Acknowledgements

Thanks are due to the following individuals and organisations for the use of illustrations and assistance: Ferrari SpA, Jonathan Flower, Washington Photo, Marcel Massini, James Allington, LAT and the Ludvigsen Library. The author and publisher are particularly grateful to Ted Walker of Ferret Fotographic.

Page iv photograph: An 850 Monza, chassis number 0602M, awaits technical verification at the retrospective Mille Miglia.

Typeset in 11/15 Baskerville.
Typesetting and origination by
Sutton Publishing Limited.
Printed and bound in England by
J.H. Haynes & Co. Ltd, Sparkford.

CONTENTS

CHRONOLOGY

1898 Enzo Ferrari born 18 February; birth registered 20 February

1919 Enzo Ferrari enters first motor race in a CMN on 5 October

1920 Enzo Ferrari becomes a member of the Alfa Romeo racing team

1923 Enzo Ferrari marries Laura Garello on 28 April, and Countess Baracca reportedly presents Enzo Ferrari with the Cavallino Rampante logo

1928 King Victor Emmanuel III bestows title Commendatore on Enzo Ferrari

1929 Scuderia Ferrari formed, and registered on 29 November

1932 Birth of Dino, son of Enzo and Laura Ferrari, on 19 January

1938 Alfa Romeo cease support of Scuderia Ferrari, and take the racing department back to Milan under the title Alfa Corse

1939 Enzo Ferrari parts company with Alfa Romeo and forms Auto Avio Costruzioni

1940 Two Auto Avio Costruzioni 815 cars produced

1945 Son Piero born to Lina Lardi on 22 May, and Gioacchino Colombo starts design work on the first Ferrari V12 engine

1946 Auto Avio Costruzioni changes name to Auto Costruzioni Ferrari

1947 First Ferrari car produced, the type 125, is victorious in its second race, the Rome Grand Prix on 25 May

1948 Biondetti/Navone win the Mille Miglia in a Ferrari 166 Allemano-bodied coupé. Ferrari displays two cars at the Turin Salon for the first time

1949 Chinetti/Selsdon win the first post-war Le Mans 24 Hour Race in a 166MM Barchetta. Two weeks later Chinetti/Lucas win the Spa 24 Hour Race in a similar car. Biondetti/Salani win the Mille Miglia in a 166MM Barchetta

1950 Inauguration of the F1 Drivers' World Championship. Marzotto/Crosara win the Mille Miglia in a 195 Touring Berlinetta

1951 Froilan Gonzalez gives Ferrari their first victory in the F1 Championship, winning the British Grand Prix at Silverstone. Villoresi/Cassani win the Mille Miglia in a 340 America Vignale Berlinetta

1952 Alberto Ascari wins the Drivers' World Championship in a Ferrari, and the Mille Miglia is won by Bracco/Rolfo in a 250 Sport Vignale Berlinetta. Ferrari win the Manufacturers' Championship

1953 Albert Ascari takes his second Drivers' World Championship title in a Ferrari, and Marzotto/Crosara repeat their 1950 victory in the Mille Miglia, this time in a 340MM Vignale Spider. Ferrari win the Manufacturers' Championship

1954 Gonzalez/Trintignant win the Le Mans 24 Hour Race in a 375 Plus. Ferrari win the Manufacturers' Championship

1956 Dino Ferrari dies on 30 June. Juan Manuel Fangio wins the F1 World Championship in a Ferrari, while in the Mille Miglia Ferraris fill the top five places, Castellotti winning in a 290MM. Ferrari win the Manufacturers' Championship

1957 Taruffi wins the last Mille Miglia in a 315S. The fatal crash of de Portago involving spectators caused the cessation of the event. Ferrari win the Manufacturers' Championship

1958 Mike Hawthorn wins the F1 World Championship in a Ferrari, and P. Hill/Gendebien in a 250 Testa Rossa win the Le Mans 24 Hour Race. Ferrari win the Manufacturers' Championship

1960 Name of the company changes to Societa Esercizio Fabbriche Automobili e Corse Ferrari, or SEFAC Ferrari. Gendebien/Frere in a 250TRI win Le Mans. Ferrari win the Manufacturers' Championship

1961 Phil Hill becomes the first American F1 World Champion in a Ferrari, with Ferrari taking the Constructors' title. Von Trips is killed in a Ferrari at Monza. The Hill/Gendebien duo in a 250TRI repeat their 1958 victory in the Le Mans 24 Hour Race. Ferrari win the Manufacturers' Championship

1962 Hill/Gendebien reach their joint hat-trick of Le Mans victories driving a Ferrari 330TRI/LM. Ferrari win the Manufacturers' Championship

1963 Bandini/Scarfiotti in a 250P win the Le Mans 24 Hour Race. Ferrari win the Manufacturers' Championship

1964 John Surtees becomes the first World Champion on both two wheels and four, driving a Ferrari, with Ferrari taking the Constructors' title. The 275P of Guichet/Vacarella wins the Le Mans 24 Hour Race. Ferrari win the Manufacturers' Championship

1965 Rindt/Gregory win the Le Mans 24 Hour Race in a 275LM, the marque's sixth consecutive win. Ferrari win the Manufacturers' Championship. Ferrari and Fiat sign an agreement for the latter to produce the V6 Dino engine

1967 Ferrari score a memorable 1–2–3 victory in the Daytona 24 Hour Race, resulting in the unofficial adoption of the title 'Daytona' for the 365GTB/4

road car. Ferrari win the Manufacturers' Championship

1969 Fiat purchase 40 per cent of Ferrari share capital, with a further 49 per cent to go to them upon the death of Enzo Ferrari, who for now retains full control over the racing department

1972 Ferrari win the Manufacturers' Championship. The Fiorano test track is opened adjacent to the factory in Maranello

1975 Niki Lauda wins the F1 World Championship in a Ferrari, with Ferrari taking the Constructors' title

1976 Ferrari win the F1 Constructors' Championship

1977 Niki Lauda wins his second F1 World Championship in a Ferrari, with Ferrari again taking the Constructors' title

1979 Jody Scheckter wins the F1 World Championship in a Ferrari, with Ferrari taking the Constructors' title

1982 Ferrari win the F1 Constructors' Championship. A new competition department is built next to the Fiorano circuit

1983 Ferrari win the F1 Constructors' Championship

1987 The former Scuderia Ferrari (later Assistenza Clienti) premises in Modena are demolished to provide a municipal car park

1988 Enzo Ferrari celebrates his 90th birthday in February, hosting a party in the factory for the entire staff. Pope John Paul II visits the Ferrari factory on 4 June. Enzo Ferrari dies on 14 August. Ferrari purchase the Mugello race circuit near Florence

1989 The company name is changed from SEFAC Ferrari to Ferrari SpA

1995 Ferrari open a site on the Internet in November, address http://www.ferrari.it

1997 Ferrari acquire 50 per cent of Maserati SpA

1999 Ferrari win the F1 Constructors' Championship, and purchase the remaining 50 per cent of shares in Maserati SpA from the parent Fiat group

INTRODUCTION

Motor racing has been the whole *raison d'être* of Ferrari as a car manufacturer, with road car production introduced as a means of paying for the racing models and the racing programme. This passion for motor sport has spanned over fifty years (or over eighty years if you include Enzo Ferrari's personal competition career), and has fascinated enthusiasts worldwide for generations, creating a fanatical following for the cars that bear the famed 'Cavallino Rampante' badge, and for those who drive them at the highest levels of motor sport. Some of the greatest and most revered names in the world of motor sport have driven for Ferrari, including 'The Flying Mantuan' Tazio Nuvolari, 'The Pampas Bull' Froilan Gonzalez, Alberto Ascari, Juan Manuel Fangio, Mike Hawthorn, Britain's first F1 World Champion, Phil Hill, the first American F1 World Champion, and John Surtees, who is still the only man to have won world championships on both two and four wheels. More recent drivers include the ebullient Gilles Villeneuve and Michael Schumacher, arguably the fastest and most naturally talented driver of the late twentieth century.

The racing road has not always been smooth for Ferrari, with numerous lean periods in terms of results (see Appendix I), but they have proved remarkably resilient, always seeking to better the team's performance and to keep fighting. In the late 1960s, for example, they were trying to compete in so many different categories that their resources, both engineering and financial, were stretched to the limit. The outcome was a lack of success where it counted, on the racetrack, with only one F1 grand prix victory in the period 1967–9. The early 1990s were similarly barren, but for different reasons, with internal wranglings creating a lack of cohesion that saw a slump in results, with only one F1 grand prix victory between 1991 and 1994 (Gerhard Berger's win in the 1994 German Grand Prix). It wasn't until 1996, when Ferrari President Luca di Montezemolo pulled everything more tightly together under a totally restructured design and management team, with Michael Schumacher as the lead driver, that the results started to improve. Since then the wins have been mounting, but so far it has been a case of always the bridesmaid but never the bride in the Driver's Championship, although there was the richly deserved reward of the Constructors' Championship in 1999.

This book looks back at the fifty-year racing history of this extraordinary company, cataloguing the principal racing cars, the single-seaters, sports racing cars, sports prototypes and GT cars which have contributed so much to motor sport all over the world. This publication is a companion volume to my earlier book *Ferrari: The Road Cars*, and it aims to offer as full an account as possible. Some of the road-going racing cars illustrated in the previous volume are also shown here as in the early years many Ferrari models were produced as dual-purpose road and competition models. It was not until the end of the 1950s that the sports racing competition models became an impractical proposition for road use, and thus delineation became simpler. Even

later, though, some of the GT cars developed primarily for competition use, such as the legendary 250GTO, the 275GTB/C and the 365GTB/4C, proved to be reliable road cars. Due to the intertwinement of road cars and sports racing models, some degree of overlap in the content of the two volumes is inevitable.

Racing has been an integral part of Ferrari from the founder's very first race on 5 October 1919, through the Scuderia Ferrari days of the 1930s and the rebirth of motor racing after the Second World War, and up to the present day. Let us hope that they will continue for many more years, so that future generations can enjoy the passions and fervour created by the most charismatic marque in the history of the automobile.

Froilan Gonzalez reacquainted with the 375 F1, the same model in which he gave Ferrari their first F1 Championship victory in 1951, here at the company's 50th anniversary celebrations in Rome in June 1997.

Chapter 1

THE FORMATIVE YEARS

In 1940 two examples of the Auto Avio Costruzioni 815 were built. They carried this name rather than 'Ferrari' because of the terms of severance of the contract between Enzo Ferrari and Alfa Romeo in force at that time. The model was based on a Fiat 508 C chassis, and basically used a number of components from two Fiat four-cylinder engines, including the cylinder heads wedded to a new cast alloy block, to form a straight-eight cylinder engine with specially machined camshaft and crankshaft. The model title '815' referred to the number of cylinders (8), and the 1.5-litre capacity of the engine (15). The two cars were entered in the 'Primo Gran Premio Brescia delle Mille Miglia' in April 1940 and showed promise, leading the 1500cc class until they retired with mechanical problems. This was their only race appearance before the hostilities of the Second World War stopped further motor racing activity.

The first car produced by Ferrari was manufactured under the Auto Avio Costruzioni label in 1940. This was necessary due to the severance terms of Enzo Ferrari's contract with Alfa Romeo in 1939, which forbade him from producing a car bearing his name for a period of four years. Two examples are known to have been constructed, and they had a straight-eight engine mounted in a modified Fiat chassis, with an all-enveloping aluminium body by Carrozzeria Touring. These two cars made their racing debut in the 1940 Mille Miglia, and led the up-to-1500cc class before retiring with mechanical ailments. By this time Great Britain and France were already at war with Germany, and motor racing soon ceased as the conflict escalated.

Upon the cessation of the Second World War in 1945, a war-ravaged Europe had to be rebuilt after the decimation of people and property during the six years of conflict. Italy had suffered as an ally of Germany, and many industrial centres had been heavily bombed. Although the Auto Avio Costruzioni (Ferrari) factory had been moved out of Modena to Maranello during the war, as part of an Italian industrial decentralisation programme, it was still bombed twice as an industrial target. Thus in 1945 Enzo Ferrari had a damaged factory producing small aero engines and machine tools with severely limited supplies of raw materials. However, even in 1945 his thoughts were focused on producing a car to take over the mantle of the AAC 815 of 1940 – he certainly didn't want to produce machine tools for the rest of his life.

To meet this aim he hired Gioacchino Colombo, an engineer whom he respected and had worked with at Alfa Romeo before the war. He commissioned Colombo to design a V12 engine to power the car he planned to build. Alfa Romeo, perhaps aware of the work that Colombo was doing for Ferrari, charged him with the responsibility of another project, thus leaving Ferrari without a chief designer. Colombo found an out-of-work colleague, Giuseppe Busso, to take over his work at Ferrari, and Aurelio Lampredi was also recruited to the design team to supervise putting the design into practice. Initially Lampredi stayed for only a short period owing to differences of opinion on design philosophy and practices, but he was lured back by Ferrari at the end of 1947 as head of design and testing, a position that he retained until 1955. He was responsible for the design of the so-called 'long block' V12 engines (which featured cylinder liners screwed into the cylinder heads, making the engine longer), as well as the very successful four-cylinder engines, and the six-cylinder derivatives.

The early efforts bore fruit as the 125 model, with a 1500cc 60-degree V12 engine. The model title '125' referred to the swept volume of a single cylinder, a practice that has subsequently featured regularly in Ferrari model designations. This car was first tested in March 1947, and made its race debut on 11 May at Piacenza, driven by Franco Cortese, where it led the race before retiring. It reappeared for the Rome Grand Prix on 25 May, again driven by Franco Cortese, and here it achieved the first ever Ferrari race victory. These first two cars were subsequently upgraded, with increased cylinder capacity, becoming the 159 and 166 models – thus neither car exists today. To fill this important gap in the history of the company, Ferrari constructed a complete replica of a 125S during the late 1980s, even manufacturing an engine of the correct type from the original drawings. This was completed in 1990, and given the chassis number 90125, in recognition of the year of completion and the model type.

Ferrari's first major race victory was achieved in May 1948 when Biondetti/ Navone won the prestigious Mille Miglia in a 166S. This was swiftly followed by a win in the Targa Florio by Biondetti, this time with Troubetzkoy as co-driver. Later in the year Luigi Chinetti and Lord Selsdon provided Ferrari with their first victory on foreign soil, when they won the Paris 12 Hour Race at the Montlhery track south of Paris in a 166 Inter model. The year 1948 also marked Ferrari's first exhibition at a major Auto Salon, when two Touring-bodied 166MMs – one a fixed-head berlinetta, the other a barchetta (Italian for small boat) – were displayed at the Turin Salon. The MM in the name was a reference to the Mille Miglia victory. The barchetta body style proved very popular, and was used on a number of Ferrari models with larger engines and longer-wheelbase chassis over the next two years, although the 166 version was the largest in terms of production numbers.

During 1949 the 166 models – in both sports racing guise as the 166MM and in single-seater form – racked up numerous victories all over Europe. Once again the Mille Miglia and Targa Florio fell to Ferrari, but perhaps the most widely recognised and prestigious win came at the first post-war Le Mans 24 Hour Race. Here Luigi Chinetti drove his most famous race. Partnered by Lord Selsdon in a 166MM, he drove for twenty-three of the twenty-four hours at an average speed of 82mph to win by one lap from the Delage driven by Louveau/Jover. However, it would be another five years before Ferrari would once

again savour victory at the Sarthe circuit. But the 1949 victory really brought Ferrari to the attention of the motoring world, and their claim to fame was driven home shortly afterwards (no pun intended) when Luigi Chinetti, partnered by Jean Lucas in another 166MM, won the Spa 24 Hour Race. The Ferrari name was now truly on the international motor sports map.

One of the most amazing aspects of this period concerned the logistics of transporting the cars to far-flung destinations. Remember, commercial road transport was much slower and less reliable than today, there was no motorway infrastructure and the roads were generally of a low standard. Yet factory-prepared Ferraris frequently took part in races in many parts of Europe. Even the task of transporting five cars, the mechanics, spares and tools to the Bari Grand Prix in southern Italy seems rather daunting in the context of the period. The passion for racing and resilience to hardship of all those involved can only be admired and applauded, and through their determination they created the Ferrari legend.

In 1950 the Formula One Drivers' Championship was created, and Ferrari contested this with the 340 and 375 F1 models featuring Lampredi-designed V12 engines; the 166-engined models contested F2 category races, and enjoyed greater success than their larger-engined relatives. The first Ferrari victory in the F1 Drivers' Championship came in July 1951, when Froilan Gonzalez won the British Grand Prix at Silverstone in a 375 F1 model, with Alberto Ascari following this up with wins in the German and Italian Grand Prix. The year 1951 also marked the first major international race victory in the 'New World', when (that man again) Luigi

Chinetti partnered Piero Taruffi to win the gruelling Carrera Panamericana Mexican road race in a 212 Inter coupé, with the similar car of Ascari/Villoresi making it a Ferrari 1–2. This adventure really brought Ferrari to the attention of the wealthy American market and opened up avenues of great potential sales, which Luigi Chinetti, as the distributor for the USA, was able to capitalise on. There were numerous other victories, including the Mille Miglia, non-championship F1 and F2 races, but none matched the commercial importance of that victory in the Carrera Panamericana. It had shown that Ferraris were not only fast but also robust and tough enough to endure and win that car-breaking marathon.

During 1952 and 1953 the Drivers' World Championship was for F2 cars with a maximum engine capacity of 2 litres. Ferrari entered their four-cylinder 500 model with its Lampredi-designed twin overhead camshaft engine, which proved to be the class of the field during both seasons, making it one of the most successful Grand Prix cars of all time. Piero Taruffi, driving a 500 F2, won the opening grand prix of the season in Switzerland, and then the great Alberto Ascari (who had missed the Switzerland race as he was competing at Indianapolis) went on to take the next nine World Championship Grand Prix in a row through 1952 and into 1953, taking the Drivers' Championship for both seasons in the process. The 500 F2 model also cleaned up in most of the non-championship races in both seasons, and Ferrari continued their winning ways in the Mille Miglia in both years.

In 1954 the Drivers' Championship was once again for F1 cars, with a maximum engine capacity of 2.5 litres. Ferrari enlarged the size of their four-cylinder engine to the new limit, and called it the 625. (Apart from the greater engine capacity, the concept was basically the same as that of the 500 F2.) Later in the season the 553 F1 model joined the Ferrari ranks, notching up a win with Mike Hawthorn in the Spanish Grand Prix. Gonzalez/Trintignant driving a 375 Plus model gave Ferrari their first Le Mans win since 1949, with Umberto Maglioli taking victory in the Carrera Panamericana with a solo drive in a similar car. However, grand prix victories would not fall as they had done in the previous two years, as Mercedes had now joined the fray with their W196 'streamliner'. This proved almost unbeatable in the hands of Juan Manuel Fangio, who went on to take the Drivers' World Championship. In 1955 the Mercedes W196 again led the way, and once again it was Juan Manuel Fangio who took the laurels in the Drivers' Championship. However, 1955 was not a good year for Mercedes: after a freak accident at Le Mans Pierre Levegh's Mercedes vaulted into the crowd, killing the driver and more than eighty spectators. About a hundred others were injured. The repercussions of this tragedy saw races cancelled, and motor racing was banned in Switzerland. Mercedes withdrew from the sport at the end of the season.

The mid-1950s proved relatively barren for Ferrari in terms of F1 victories, and it was not until they 'inherited' the works Lancia D50s for the 1956 season that there was a reversal of fortunes. With Mercedes' withdrawal, Juan Manuel Fangio joined Ferrari to drive the Lancia-Ferrari D50. This car and driver combination proved very successful, with Fangio taking his third consecutive Drivers' title. This was largely due to the generosity of his English team-mate Peter Collins, who would have won the title himself had he not handed over his car to Fangio after the latter's car had broken down in the last Grand Prix of the season at Monza in Italy. In the 1956 Mille Miglia Ferraris were dominant, filling the top five places, and they were also victorious in the Sebring 12 Hour Race and the Swedish rounds of the Sports Car World Championship to take the title. The new Ferrari 250GT berlinetta took victory in the Tour de France Auto driven by de Portago/Nelson. The run of success for the 250GT models in this event would continue without interruption until 1964, a remarkable winning sequence in a hard-fought annual contest. It was in 1956 that Enzo Ferrari lost his son Dino, who died on 30 June at the age of just twenty-four. His death had a profound and lasting effect on his father, who gradually became more reclusive, rarely leaving the Modena area.

In 1957 Fangio moved to Maserati and although the Lancia-Ferraris were still competitive they couldn't stop him taking his fourth consecutive (and fifth in total) F1 Drivers' Championship. In the Mille Miglia Ferrari experienced both ends of the spectrum, with Taruffi's victory overshadowed by de Portago's fatal accident (which also claimed the life of his co-driver and eleven spectators). This led to the Italian government imposing a ban on racing on public roads, and the end of the famous road race. Further wins in Argentina and Venezuela, together with a second place at the Nurburgring, meant that Ferrari once again won the Sports Car World Championship.

The year 1958 again saw triumph and tragedy for Ferrari, with Mike Hawthorn in a Dino 246 winning the Drivers' World Championship by a single point from Stirling Moss, becoming in the process Britain's first World Champion. At the end of the season he announced his retirement, only to die in a road accident a few months later. His team-mate Peter Collins did not even see the end of the season, as two weeks after winning his home grand prix at Silverstone he was killed in an accident during the German Grand Prix at the Nurburgring. In the World Sports Car Championship it was the year of the 250 Testa Rossa, in pontoon fender body form, which designer and builder Sergio Scaglietti considers to be his most beautiful creation, eclipsing even the legendary 250GTO that came later. With this model Ferrari took the manufacturers' title for the third successive year, including wins in the Targa Florio and the Le Mans 24 Hour Race on the way.

The final year of the decade saw an ebb in Ferrari fortunes, both in Formula One and in the sports car arena. In Formula One the front-engined Grand Prix car started to be eclipsed by the mid-engined Cooper, a design that literally turned single-seater racing – and subsequently sports car racing – on its head, establishing a design format that continues today. Ferrari scored two victories during the F1 season, both on high-speed circuits where top speed was more important than handling, and both times the driver was Tony Brooks in the Dino 246. Although Ferrari started the sports car season with a 1–2 victory in the Sebring 12 Hour Race, that would be the only one of the year, with Aston Martin's DBR1 model proving to be the dominant force, with a 1–2 victory at Le Mans and victory in the overall championship. The 250GTs continued their dominance of the Tour de France Auto, taking their fourth consecutive victory, which was some consolation in an otherwise uninspiring season.

The 125S, built in 1947, was the first car to carry a Ferrari badge, with the model number referring to the swept volume of a single cylinder in cubic centimetres. Thus the total capacity of the V12 engine was 1500cc. This was a practice used for many years by Ferrari to designate model types and is still sometimes employed today. A 125S model led its first race in 1947 before retiring, but was successful on its second outing in the Rome GP where Franco Cortese drove to victory on 25 May 1947. The original examples were developed into the succeeding 159S and 166S models, and neither exists today. The example pictured here is a late 1980s factory reconstruction which was completed in 1990 and appropriately carries chassis number 90125.

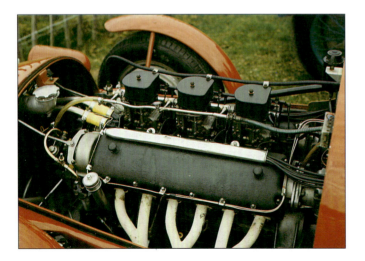

(Opposite) The 166 Spider Corsa was raced during 1948 and 1949 and featured a narrow two-seater body with cycle wings. The cut-away cockpit sides were necessary so that two occupants could be accommodated within the minimal cockpit dimensions. The engine (left) was a 2-litre V12 unit with either a single or triple carburettors and magneto ignition, producing a claimed 130bhp. There were also similarly powered 166 Sport models with fully enclosed bodywork by Allemano, and these models provided Ferrari with their first major race victories. Biondetti/Troubetzkoy won the 1948 Targa Florio in a spider version, and Biondetti/Navone won the 1948 Mille Miglia in a coupé example. The 166 Spider Corsa shown here is chassis number 002C.

(Opposite) The 166MM barchetta ('little boat') had bodywork designed by Carrozzeria Touring of Milan to their 'Superleggera' principle, using a thin aluminium body over a multitude of small tubes as a support frame. A closed roof berlinetta version was also produced, and on some examples the original 2-litre V12 engine was increased in bore size to '195' specification, to provide a cubic capacity of 2431cc. The MM in the model name is a celebration of the 1948 Mille Miglia victory by a 166 model. It is arguably one of the most beautiful of the early Ferrari models, and was first displayed at the Turin Salon of 1948. The body style was also used on larger-engined Ferrari models up to 1952. It was also very successful on the race track, with Chinetti/Selsdon winning the 1949 Le Mans 24 Hour Race, and two weeks later Chinetti/Lucas won the Spa 24 Hour Race in a similar model. These results really put Ferrari's name on the international motor racing map. The examples shown here are (top) chassis number 0010M in its Spa 24 Hour winning livery, and (bottom) Alberto Ascari's car pictured at Silverstone in 1950.

(Below) The 125 F1 was the first Ferrari monoposto (single-seater) model produced, and made its race debut in the Italian Grand Prix in 1948. The 1500cc V12 engine was fitted with a Roots-type single-stage supercharger. The regulations in force at the time permitted a supercharged engine of up to 1.5-litre capacity, or a 4.5-litre normally aspirated unit. In 1.5-litre supercharged form the engine never fulfilled its potential. This was unsurprising really, as it was a completely new design in the early stages of development. Of the three examples entered in that first race in Turin, Raymond Sommer finished third and the cars of Bira and Farina retired. The model scored its first victory in a Formula Libre race on the Garda circuit later in the year. It continued to be developed through 1949 and 1950, with numerous modifications, including a two-stage supercharger, and a four-speed De Dion transaxle on the mechanical side, while the body shape evolved from one very similar to the original 166 F2 and FL cars to the more modern and streamlined version shown here.

The 166 F2 and FL single-seater models were produced concurrently with the 125 F1 model, and the first example appeared three weeks after the debut of the 125 F1 car on 26 September 1948. The occasion was the Gran Premio di Firenze, where Raymond Sommer took the new 166 F2 model to victory on its maiden outing. The 166 single-seater models were produced in Formula 2 form with a normally aspirated 2-litre V12 engine, or in a Formula Libre version where the engine was fitted with a supercharger. As with the 125 F1, the bodywork was frequently modified during its competition career, although the 166 FL example shown here, at the 1997 Monaco Historic Grand Prix, chassis number 011F, is in its original configuration.

Period shots of 166 F2 models in action. The early-bodied car (top) is that of Frank Dobson at Ibsley in April 1952 and the later-bodied example (below) is that of Peter Hirt taking part in the International Trophy at Silverstone the same year. (Right) Plug change on Frank Dobson's 166 F2 at Boreham Airfield in June 1952. The twin magneto ignition, camshaft cover with cast Ferrari script and triple carburettor set-up are clearly evident.

(Opposite) Due to the relatively high fuel consumption and disappointing performance of the 1.5-litre supercharged F1 cars, engineer Aurelio Lampredi designed a large-capacity V12 engine. This first appeared in 1950 in 275 (3.3 litre) and 340 (4.1 litre) forms; exploiting the maximum capacity allowed by the regulations it went on to become the 375 F1, with a 4.5-litre normally aspirated engine, in time for the Italian Grand Prix that year. In the race Alberto Ascari's car retired with mechanical problems but he took over Serafini's car and finished second. It was in a 375 F1 that Froilan Gonzalez gave Ferrari their first World Championship victory, when he won the 1951 British Grand Prix at Silverstone. At the end of the season the regulations changed, and only Formula 2 cars were eligible for World Championship races in 1952 and 1953. Thus the 375 single-seater was confined to the Formula Libre races that often supported the grand prix, although an 'Indy' version was developed to contest the prestigious Indianapolis 500 race in the United States. The example shown here is 375 F1, chassis number 2, as it appeared at the Coys Historic Festival at Silverstone in 1998. (Inset) Froilan Gonzalez in a 375 F1 at the French Grand Prix in 1951, where he finished second, two weeks before his maiden GP win for Ferrari in the British Grand Prix.

The 195S Berlinetta with bodywork by Carrozzeria Touring was basically very similar to the 166MM models but was fitted with a larger-bore version of the V12 engine (65mm instead of 60mm, with the same 58.8mm stroke) to provide a cubic capacity of 2431cc. A 195S model was driven to victory in the 1950 Mille Miglia by Marzotto/Crosara. This is chassis number 0060M.

The 212 F1 model was a normally aspirated development of the 166 single-seater series produced in 1951. It was fitted with a 2563cc V12 engine fed by triple twin-choke carburettors with twin magneto ignition, mated to a de Dion transaxle. This was basically the same engine that was used in the 212 series of berlinettas, coupés and spiders for both road and sports racing use, although they were fitted with coil and distributor ignition and had a standard gearbox location with a rigid rear axle. The Swiss driver Rudi Fischer used a 2-litre example in Formula 2 races. The car pictured is chassis number 102 F1/F2.

The 212 Inter model was essentially the roadgoing 212 series model, although a number were used in competition. The engine was a 2563cc V12 unit fitted with either a single or triple twin-choke carburettors, mated to a five-speed gearbox with a rigid rear axle. They were produced in a wide range of different body styles by most of the leading Italian Carrozzeria. In fact this model has the widest range of styles, by the greatest number of designers, of any Ferrari model built. The coupé examples shown are by Touring, chassis number 0215EL (above), and Vignale, chassis number 0111S (below).

As with the 212 Inter models, the Export examples were fitted with a variety of bodies. This picture, taken before the start of the 1951 Le Mans 24 Hour Race, shows two 212 Export models, number 31 on the left with a Touring barchetta body, and number 29 in the centre with a Vignale coupé body. The former finished sixteenth, and the latter ninth.

The 212 Export was ostensibly the sports racing model of the 212 series. However, some examples like the Vignale cabriolet (left), chassis number 0106E, were obviously intended only for road use despite having an even series competition chassis number. Conversely the Vignale spider (below) carries much more sporting-orientated bodywork on chassis number 0182ED.

The 340 America was the first sports Ferrari to be fitted with the large-capacity Lampredi-designed 'long block' V12 engine with a total capacity of 4.1 litres. The design featured cylinder liners screwed into the cylinder heads which increased the space between the bores, hence the 'long block' description, which differentiated it from the smaller-capacity Colombo-designed V12 engines. The example shown, chassis number 0082A, won the 1951 Mille Miglia driven by Villoresi/Cassani.

The changed regulations adopted by the governing body for 1952, after the withdrawal of Alfa Romeo from F1 at the end of the 1951 season, meant that the World Championship was only open to F2 cars. Accordingly, Ferrari produced their first four-cylinder engine. This was the 2-litre twin overhead camshaft type 500, with a concurrent 2.5-litre type 625 engine suitable for Formula Libre racing. The new four-cylinder engine proved to be lighter than the V12 166 unit, with fewer reciprocating parts. It was also more powerful and had greater torque, and thus it came to be fitted in the 500 F2 car, Ferrari's great hope for the 1952 World Championship season. This is Alberto Ascari's victorious car in the Silverstone paddock at the 1952 British Grand Prix. He won six of the seven grand prix that season, convincingly winning the World Championship.

The engine of the all-conquering 500 F2 model (above), in the car driven by Mike Hawthorn at Silverstone in May 1953. This engine is unusually fitted with four single-choke carburettors instead of the normal pair of twin-choke units, as seen on the 625 F1 engine below. Further differences can be seen in the shape of the camshaft covers and the angle between them, while the twin magnetos are horizontal on the 500 F2 unit and vertical on this 625 F1 example.

(Above) The 250 Sport was the predecessor to the 250MM model, which received the MM (Mille Miglia) letters in its name to commemorate the 250 Sport's victory in the 1952 Mille Miglia driven by Bracco/Rolfo. Here the 250S Vignale berlinetta of Ascari/Villoresi leads the similarly bodied 340 America of Simon/Vincent in the 1952 Le Mans 24 Hour Race. The 250S retired, while the 340 America was the only Ferrari to finish, out of the seven that started the race.

(Opposite top) The 225S was built in 1952 with a larger-bore version of the 212 Inter engine with a total cubic capacity of 2715cc, which was fitted with coil and distributor ignition and triple twin-choke carburettors. The bodywork was either coupé or spider by Vignale, although one example received a Touring barchetta body. The 1952 Monaco Grand Prix was open to sports cars, and was won by Vittorio Marzotto in a 225S Vignale spider. The example shown is a Vignale spider, chassis number 0192ET.

(Opposite bottom) The engine bay of 225S chassis number 0192ET, with the centre of the vee dominated by the triple twin-choke carburettors and their air-filter housings.

The 340 Mexico model powered by the 4.1-litre Lampredi-designed V12 engine was built in a small series of four cars with Vignale bodywork. These cars – one spider and three berlinettas – were built specifically to compete in the demanding Mexican Carrera Panamericana road race in 1952, hence 'Mexico' appears in the model title. Only the three berlinettas actually started, and just one survived to the finish, the Chinetti/Lucas car finishing third behind a pair of works Mercedes 300SLs. This view of chassis number 0226AT show the flat-sided wing lines, with the prominent frontal protuberance on either side of the grille, and small fins at the back that flow gently into the rear lights.

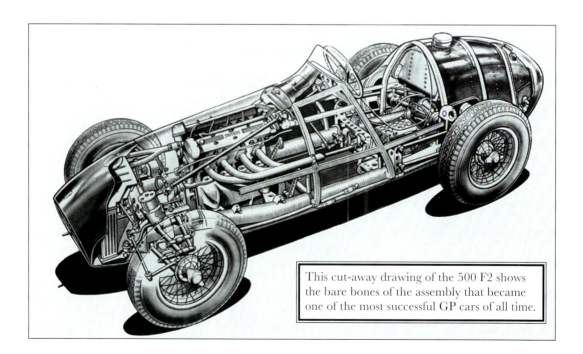

This cut-away drawing of the 500 F2 shows the bare bones of the assembly that became one of the most successful GP cars of all time.

The 500 F2 continued its winning ways through 1953 with Alberto Ascari (right) taking his second World Championship title. This was the pit lane at the British Grand Prix at Silverstone, with the 500 F2s of Villoresi and Farina in the foreground. Here Alberto Ascari took his second consecutive British Grand Prix win, while for Ferrari it was three in a row. Note the revised exhaust system compared to the 1952 car (see p. 18).

Tony Vandervell developed two Thinwall Specials in England. The first was based on a 125 F1 and the second on a 375 F1, which is shown here in the Grand Prix supporting Formula Libre race at Silverstone in 1953 driven by Farina. This car, chassis number 010, has been part of the Donington Collection for a number of years.

The second series of 166MM models, built during 1953, are generally referred to as the 166MM/53 or Series II. The normal attire was a Vignale spider body, but there were also berlinetta and coupé models from the same pen, plus a pair of Autodromo spiders, an Abarth spider and a Pinin Farina berlinetta. The Vignale spider body style was also worn by the 250MM, 340MM and 625TF models of the period, making individual identification difficult. The 166MM was built on a 2200mm wheelbase, the 250MM on a 2400mm wheelbase, and the 340MM on a 2500mm one, but unless you have a tape measure or know the particular car, then it is difficult to tell the difference visually. This is chassis number 0342M.

The 250MM model was available either as a Pinin Farina berlinetta or a Vignale spider or berlinetta, and was produced during 1953. It was a development of the 250 Sport of 1952, and fitted with a similar 3-litre V12 engine based on the original Colombo design, fitted with a bank of three quad-choke carburettors and coil and distributor ignition. The body style of the Pinin Farina berlinetta was based on the design that they used to clothe their first competition-bodied Ferrari, the 342 America model with chassis number 0236MM. These views of a Pinin Farina berlinetta, chassis number 0270MM (top), and a Vignale spider, chassis number 0274MM (below), show the different design philosophies of the two houses. Some Vignale examples received bodywork similar in style to that used on their 225S spider, but the rounded shape shown here was the usual fitment.

As with the concurrently produced 250MM model, the 340MM was available with bodywork designed by either Pinin Farina or Vignale, in styles very similar to that of its smaller-engined relative, while two examples received spider bodies by Touring. The 340MM used the 'long block' Lampredi-designed V12 engine with a total cubic capacity of 4102cc, fitted with triple quad-choke carburettors and coil and distributor ignition. The 250MM was fitted with a five-speed gearbox, but the 340MM had a four-speed unit. This is the 1953 Mille Miglia-winning Vignale spider, chassis number 0280AM.

This is a Carrozzeria Touring barchetta version of the 340MM on chassis number 0284AM.

The 375MM models were an evolution of the 340MM, with the bore of the V12 engine increased to 84mm, allied to the same stroke of 68mm. This gave a total cubic capacity of 4522cc; fitted with magneto ignition and triple quad-choke carburettors, this produced a claimed 340bhp. The bodywork was either a berlinetta or spider by Pinin Farina, or a spider by Scaglietti. There were also three one-off roadgoing coupés produced in 1954, two by Pinin Farina and one by Ghia. Shown here are a pair of Pinin Farina spiders, chassis numbers 0370AM and 0376AM, the former finished in the white and blue American racing colour scheme as raced by Masten Gregory, and the latter in the livery that it wore in the 1954 Carrera Panamericana Mexican road race. The lower picture shows a Pinin Farina berlinetta, chassis number 0368AM.

This is 375MM chassis number 0370AM competing at Goodwood in September 1954 in the hands of the owner Masten Gregory.

The engine bay of 375MM chassis number 0370AM, dominated by the camshaft covers and aluminium carburettor cold air box, with the angled twin magnetos clearly visible at the rear of the engine.

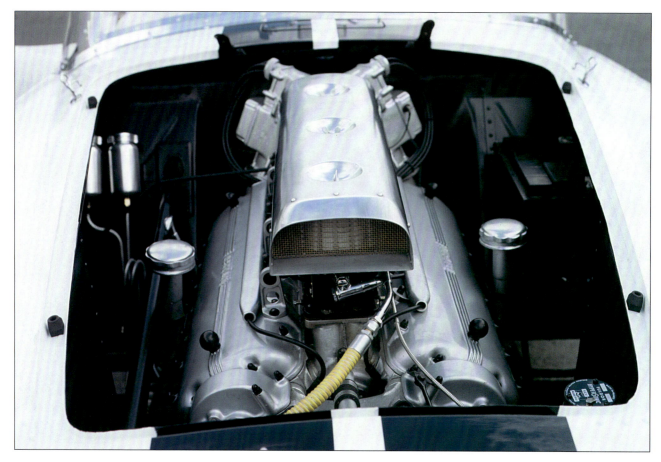

The 1953 625TF Vignale spider was the first sports racing Ferrari to be fitted with a four-cylinder engine. The unit was essentially that of the concurrent Formula One car, with a cubic capacity of 2500cc, twin overhead camshafts, two dual-choke carburettors plus twin coil and distributor ignition, to produce a claimed 220bhp. The example shown, chassis number 0304TF, is the only known survivor of the two examples built, and it can be seen that the body style is very similar to the 166MM/53, 250MM and 340MM models of the same period.

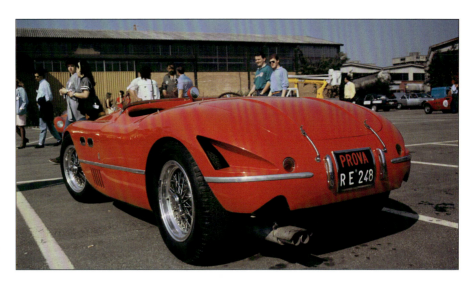

Three examples of the 735S model were built in 1953. This is Mackay Fraser's car, with Pinin Farina spider body, pictured at the Oulton Park circuit in 1956. This was the second Ferrari sports racing car to be fitted with a four-cylinder engine, which had a cubic capacity of 2.941 litres, with twin overhead camshafts, two dual-choke carburettors plus twin coil and distributor ignition, to produce a claimed 225bhp.

When the new Formula One regulations were introduced in 1954, they provided for normally aspirated engines up to 2500cc capacity, or 750cc maximum capacity supercharged engines. The 625 F1 model had been developed alongside the visually similar 500 F2, and the 2.5-litre capacity engine had been tried in Formula Libre races and the sports racing cars, thus this was to be Ferrari's weapon in the 1954 Championship season. The arrival of Mercedes in Formula One, with a team led by Fangio, upset Ferrari's chances of repeating their success with the 500 F2 during 1952 and 1953. The 625 F1 was a competitive car, but Fangio in the Mercedes was almost unstoppable as he went on to take the World Championship, ahead of the three Ferrari team drivers Gonzalez, Hawthorn and Trintignant.

(Opposite top) The 250 Europa GT was presented at the 1954 Paris Salon, and was the first model in the 250GT series that would form the backbone of Ferrari production for the next ten years. The majority of examples produced were for road use, although some had aluminium bodies and saw competition action. A small number of aluminium-bodied berlinetta variants were also produced, which are generally considered as the forerunners to the 'Tour de France' series of berlinettas. The body style was slightly different on each one, but was essentially a mix of the preceding Pinin Farina 250MM berlinetta, and what would become the first series of 'TdF' berlinettas. The engine used was a 3000cc V12 based on the original Colombo design, producing a claimed 220bhp. The berlinetta shown is chassis number 0385GT.

(Opposite bottom) The 250 Monza was produced in 1954 utilising the chassis of the four-cylinder 750 Monza and the 250 series V12 engine. The body was either a Pinin Farina spider similar in style to the 375MM, or a Scaglietti spider with a body style similar to their 500 Mondial and 750 Monza versions. As with a number of early Ferraris, they were frequently rebodied, and this example, chassis number 0432M, wears a Scaglietti rebody in the style of the 1958 pontoon fender 250 Testa Rossa.

The 375 Plus was the final development of the 375MM model, with an increase in engine capacity to 4954cc, using the same 84mm bore with a longer stroke of 74.5mm, producing a claimed 330bhp. A Pinin Farina spider body was used for the sports racing models, as seen in this picture of chassis number 0394AM, who also bodied a special cabriolet example for King Leopold of Belgium, while Scaglietti also produced a spider example that was subsequently modified by Sutton. Driving solo, Umberto Maglioli won the 1954 Carrera Panamericana road race in a 375 Plus, while the Le Mans 24 Hour Race earlier that year went to Gonzalez/Trintignant in a similar model.

The 500 Mondial was the last competition sports racing spider designed by Pinin Farina, with a smaller-scale version of the body used on the 375MM, although the majority of examples had spider bodies designed and built by Scaglietti. The Lampredi-designed engine was a four-cylinder 2-litre double overhead camshaft unit, with a pair of twin-choke side-draught carburettors and two sparking plugs per cylinder. The car pictured is the Scaglietti-bodied chassis number 0454MD.

The 750 Monza shared a very similar body style to the 500 Mondial, while the engine was a 3-litre derivation of the Lampredi four-cylinder unit, hence the '750' single-cylinder swept capacity designation in the model title. Along with the smaller-engined 500 Mondial, it was produced between 1954 and 1956. Many are still used actively in historic racing, such as chassis number 0552M, seen here at Monaco in 1997.

Although the 625 F1 continued in partial service during the 1955 F1 season, the 553 model had been developed during 1954 and evolved into the 555 Squalo and Supersqualo models, taking over completely from the 625 during the early part of 1955. Against the continuing dominance of Fangio and Mercedes, plus the powerful Lancia D50s, the 555 didn't win a single F1 grand prix. It is seen here driven by Paul Frere in the 1955 Belgian Grand Prix on his way to fourth place.

Ferrari inherited the 2.5-litre V8-engined Lancia D50 towards the end of the 1955 season when financial pressures forced Lancia to leave the racing scene. Mercedes also withdrew from motor racing at the end of the year in the aftermath of the 1955 Le Mans race tragedy, and so Fangio did not have his 'silver arrow' for 1956. But he knew where the strongest competition had come from in 1955, and who had the best cars now – and thus it was to Ferrari that he went for the 1956 season. Ably assisted by his team-mates, he went on to collect his fourth World Championship crown.

For the 1956 season the Lancia D50 was rebadged as a Ferrari and called the Lancia-Ferrari. This rather oversimplifies the case, as numerous modifications were carried out, including revisions to the chassis so that the engine was no longer a stressed member and relocation of the fuel tanks from the panniers to behind the driver. This is the Ecurie Francorchamps-entered example of Andre Pillette in the 1956 Belgian Grand Prix, on its way to sixth place. The filler for the relocated fuel tank can be clearly seen behind the driver's head.

During 1955 Ferrari produced the 118LM, their first sports racing model powered by a straight-six engine, with a body very similar to the 500 Mondial/750 Monza models (albeit the chassis was 150mm longer to accommodate the additional length of the six-cylinder engine). Initially the engine capacity was 3.75 litres, but it was soon increased to 4.4 litres, with the model name being the 121LM. This was a short-lived experiment and the models had no great success. This is the 121LM, chassis number 0558, of Maglioli and Phil Hill at Le Mans in 1955, where it retired (along with all the other Ferraris entered).

The ranks of the four-cylinder Ferraris were swollen in 1955 with the announcement of the 857S Monza with a 3.43-litre engine. This became the 860 Monza model in 1956. The Scaglietti-built bodies were not as slim as those of their smaller-engined namesake, with a deeper, more rounded radiator grille bounded by brake cooling holes, and the wheelbase of the chassis was 100mm longer. This is an 860 Monza chassis, number 0602M.

The 250GT berlinetta of 1956 was the first in a series of 250GT berlinetta models that came to dominate their class in GT racing, and vied for overall honours for almost a decade. The 3-litre V12 engine was developed from that fitted in the preceding 250 Europa GT series, driving through a four-speed gearbox to a rigid rear axle. The example shown is chassis number 0539GT. All cars in the series had aluminium bodies constructed by Scaglietti, and were left-hand-drive. After victory in the 1956 Tour de France Ferrari won the right to use the event name in the model title, and the series that followed became known as the 250GT Tour de France (TdF) berlinettas.

(Opposite top) The 290MM sports racing model was manufactured in a small series of four cars in 1956, with open spider bodywork by Scaglietti. They were fitted with a 3491cc V12 engine, with either triple or six twin-choke carburettors with quadruple coil and distributor ignition, producing a claimed 320bhp. The example pictured, chassis number 0616MM, was the winner of the 1956 Mille Miglia driven by Eugenio Castellotti.

(Opposite bottom) The 410S was the second V12-engined sports racing model produced by Ferrari during 1956. As with the 290MM, only four examples were made, three with Scaglietti spider bodies and the fourth, chassis number 0594CM pictured here, with a berlinetta version of the same body. The V12 engine was of 4961.6cc capacity, coupled to a five-speed transaxle, producing a claimed 340bhp.

Apart from the two V12-engined sports racing models and the four-cylinder 860 Monza, Ferrari introduced another four-cylinder model in 1956, the 500 Testa Rossa, so named because of its red-painted cam covers. This is the car (number 22), chassis number 0654MDTR, of Picard/Tappan pictured before the start of the 1956 Le Mans 24 Hour Race, in which it was disqualified for a refuelling infringement while leading its class. The three cars behind it are 625LM variants of the model.

(Left) The 625LM was a 2.5-litre variant of the 500TR sports racing model, also produced during 1956. The example shown is the works-entered car of Gendebien/ Trintignant, chassis number 0644MDTR, during the 1956 Le Mans 24 Hour Race. Of the six Ferraris that started, this was the only one to finish, taking a creditable third place.

For 1957 the Lancia-Ferrari was developed into the type 801 model ('8' for the number of cylinders and '01' for Formula One), a change to the normal Ferrari model type designation. Although the capacity remained at 2.5 litres, the engine of the 801 had a larger bore and shorter stroke, producing a claimed 275bhp. Fangio had moved to Maserati to drive their 250F model, with which he went on to take his fifth World Drivers' Championship. The Ferrari 801 had wins in three non-championship races, but none in the World Championship itself. These pictures show Mike Hawthorn in the 801 at Rouen in the French Grand Prix, car number 14, where he finished fourth, and in the German Grand Prix at the Nurburgring where he was second.

The 250GT Tour de France model was provided with a revised body style for 1957. The major changes were to the rear section, where the rear screen size was reduced, the wing profile changed, and a fourteen-louvre 'sail panel' vent arrangement provided. Later in the year the front wing line was changed and the headlights were mounted higher under perspex covers, while the sail panel vent arrangement changed to a three-louvre design. This is an early 1957 model, chassis number 0607GT, being driven by Wolfgang Seidel at the Nurburgring in the grand prix support race, which it won.

The Bridgehampton circuit (USA) in September 1957. In the foreground is the 290MM spider, chassis number 0616, of 'Honest' John Kilborn; car number 42 is the 315S model, chassis number 0684, of William Greenspun. Note the similarity in body style, and the subtle differences.

For the 1957 sports racing season Ferrari produced two twelve-cylinder models, the first of which was the 315S. This had a 3.78-litre V12 engine with 76mm x 69.5mm bore and stroke, and was fitted with a bank of six twin-choke carburettors, with twin coil and distributor ignition, mated to a four-speed transaxle, producing a claimed 360bhp. A 315S driven by Piero Taruffi won the last Mille Miglia in 1957. The road race was stopped after this running after the fatal accident involving de Portago's similar car, in which the driver, co-driver and a number of spectators perished. As shown here, chassis number 0656 was rebodied in the style of the pontoon-fendered 250 Testa Rossa in 1958, but has since been returned to its original body configuration.

The second V12 model, the 335S, appeared a little later in the year. Visually very similar to the 315S, it had a similar engine and transmission layout, but with an increased bore and stroke of 77mm x 72mm to provide an engine capacity of 4023cc, with a claimed power output of 390bhp. This is chassis number 0700, wearing the mandatory weather equipment necessitated by the regulations in force at that time.

The third sports racing model for the 1957 season was the four-cylinder 500TRC, which was a development of the 500TR of 1956, with the 'C' suffix relating to the Group C regulations then in force (governing the specification of the cars that raced in this class). This is chassis number 0690MDTR, which was driven by Markleson in the 1960 Cuban Grand Prix. Note the armed soldier strolling down the pit lane to the left of the car.

(Opposite) During 1956 Ferrari had been working on a V6 engine project, which resulted in a 1500cc Formula 2 car that first raced in early 1957. Enzo Ferrari has always given the credit for the inception of the project to his son Dino, who had died in 1956, before completing work on the project with the talented engineer Vittorio Jano. The capacity of the engine was increased in stages until it reached 2.417 litres, to power the 246 F1 car for the 1958 season. Mike Hawthorn won the 1958 Drivers' World Championship in the 246 by a single point, after a season-long battle with Stirling Moss. This was the inaugural year of the Constructors' Championship, where Ferrari finished second to Vanwall. The 246 continued to be the Ferrari weapon in the F1 battlefield for 1959 and 1960. However, on all but the fastest circuits it was outclassed by the new generation of mid-engined cars pioneered by Cooper, a design that was swiftly followed by other British manufacturers. Tony Brooks gave the 246 two wins during 1959, in the French Grand Prix at Reims and in the German Grand Prix at the Avus circuit (as seen here). The model's final victory came in the 1960 Italian Grand Prix at Monza, where Phil Hill led a Ferrari 1–2–3, in a race boycotted by the other major teams.

A single 246 F1 car was fitted with a 3-litre V12 engine for use in the Tasman series. This was chassis number 0007/0788, pictured here.

The 250GT Tour de France model changed very little for the 1958 season, the main visual difference being the adoption of a single vent louvre on the sail panel. Otherwise it was business as usual with numerous GT category victories, including a third consecutive Tour de France victory, with 250GT berlinettas filling the top five places. This is a typical 1958 example competing in the Freiburg Hillclimb in 1959.

(Opposite top) The sports racing models for the 1958 season were reduced from the plethora of different configurations of the preceding years to basically a single model, the 250 Testa Rossa, although a unique 412 Monza was built to contest the Los Angeles Times Grand Prix at Riverside. This was powered by a 4023cc V12 engine and its body style and running gear were similar to those of the 315S and 335S cars of 1957. The 250 Testa Rossa was powered by a 3-litre V12 engine based on that used in the 250GT series, but with many lighter parts, and fitted with a bank of six twin-choke carburettors to produce a claimed power output of 290bhp (30bhp more than that claimed for the 250GT TdF berlinetta). Sergio Scaglietti considers the pontoon-fendered Testa Rossa as his most beautiful creation – judging by the number of earlier Ferraris that were rebodied in the style, he was not alone in his thoughts. Although the pontoon-fender nose treatment was beautiful, it was found to cause high-speed lift, and was modified on the works entries for Le Mans to a more normal all-enveloping configuration. Phil Hill and Olivier Gendebien took the first of their three joint Le Mans victories in one of these cars. The example shown is the original pontoon-fender style on chassis number 0718TR.

(Opposite bottom) The 250GT Tour de France berlinetta entered the final stage of its development in 1959. Initially the body was very similar to the 1958 model, with the exception of the headlights that became open units mounted in shallow recesses in the wing extremities. This was due to new lighting legislation in Italy, although cars sold outside Italy could still be provided with the covered light arrangement if the owner wished. The last of the series, produced from the middle of 1959, were fitted with a completely different style of body, that would be continued in slightly modified form into the 1960 series of berlinettas. These last cars are now frequently referred to as 'interim' berlinettas. They can be identified by the small quarter window in the sail panel behind the door glass, as seen here on chassis number 1509GT, which the later SWB berlinettas did not have.

Nurburgring, 1958. Mike Hawthorn refuels the 250 Testa Rossa while the mechanics change the rear wheels. Note the shredded tyre lying to the left rear of the car, which brought him into the pits, losing him (and Peter Collins) the lead.

Apart from the standard Scaglietti-bodied series of 2600mm wheelbase 250GT berlinettas produced between 1956 and 1959, there were also five examples produced with varying bodywork styled and constructed by Zagato. The car pictured is chassis number 0537GT that features the famed Zagato 'double bubble' roofline.

The 250 GT California spider, in both long- and short-wheelbase forms, was essentially a road car. However, it did have the occasional foray into competition, notably at Sebring in 1959 and 1960 where a class win was gained each time, and at Le Mans in 1959 and 1960. This is chassis number 1459GT, the 1960 Sebring class-winning car that finished 8th overall.

The 250TR/59 was the evolution of the 1958 Testa Rossa model for the 1959 season, now fitted with a spider body designed and built by Fantuzzi in Modena. It won the first race of the Worlds Sports Car Championship season at the Sebring 12 Hour Race, but thereafter the season was dominated by the Aston Martin DBR1 that won the title. The example pictured is chassis number 0768TR, driven by Pete Lovely at Sebring in 1961.

Chapter 2

THE 1960s

Although Ferrari continued with the front-engined Dino 246 for the 1960 F1 season, they also fielded this mid-engined car, the Dino 246P, in that year's Monaco Grand Prix. Driven by Richie Ginther, it finished in sixth place. It made only one further appearance, when it was driven to fifth place in the Italian Grand Prix by Wolfgang von Trips.

The arrival of the new decade saw nothing really new from Ferrari. They continued with the Dino 246 in Formula One, although they did produce an experimental mid-engined Dino 246P that only raced twice, in the Monaco and Italian Grand Prix. In the sports car field the successful 250 Testa Rossa was further developed, and with the withdrawal of Aston Martin from the fray after their 1959 championship victory, it was a straight fight between Ferrari and Porsche, although Moss/Gurney provided Maserati with a victory in the Nurburgring 1000km Race. Because of the points scoring system, where only the best three results counted, Ferrari and Porsche were tied on points at the end of the season, but the championship was awarded to Ferrari because their overall points tally was greater than Porsche's.

By 1961 the pendulum had swung, and with the new 1.5-litre engine capacity limit the F1 grids were a mid-engined monopoly. Ferrari introduced their famous 156 'shark nose' mid-engined car, fitted with either a 65 or 120 degree V6 engine, to do battle with the other main protagonists – Cooper, Lotus and Porsche. The season bore witness to two epic battles that are ingrained in the annals of motor sport history. The first of these was the Monaco Grand Prix, where Stirling Moss in Rob Walker's privately entered Lotus 18 successfully resisted all the efforts of the three chasing Ferrari drivers and recorded probably his most hard-fought and famous victory. The second battle was at the French Grand Prix, where the little-known Italian Giancarlo Baghetti appeared in a loaned Ferrari 156 after taking two non-championship victories in the Syracuse and Naples Grand Prix. After all three Ferrari team drivers retired, it was left to Baghetti to uphold Ferrari honour on the super-fast Reims circuit. Over the final few laps it came down to an enthralling slipstreaming battle between the relatively inexperienced Baghetti and the works Porsche duo of Jo Bonnier and Dan Gurney. Shortly before the end of the race the Bonnier Porsche retired and it was a straight fight between Ferrari and Porsche, with Baghetti claiming victory by 0.1 second, to claim his place in the Ferrari hall of fame.

Another event of the season is remembered for a different reason: the horrific crash in the Italian Grand Prix at Monza. In the early laps of the race the Ferrari of Wolfgang von Trips and the Lotus of Jim Clark touched, and the Ferrari was launched into the air; it scythed through a spectator enclosure, killing the driver and fourteen people. Phil Hill went on to win the race, in the process becoming the first American World Champion, and clinching the Constructors' Championship for Ferrari. With victory in every round but one, Ferrari also took the World Sports Car Championship for the second year running.

In November 1961 there was a mass exodus of senior design staff from Ferrari, including Giotto Bizzarrini and Carlo Chiti, together with team manager Romolo Tavoni, the reasons for which have never been fully disclosed (and probably never will be). This left the young but very talented engineer Mauro Forghieri in charge of design and development for the 1962 season. It was to be a year of mixed fortunes for Ferrari. They didn't record a single grand prix victory as the new V8 BRM and Coventry Climax engines dominated Formula One, but in the World Sports Car Championship run for GT cars (while the

Speed World Challenge was inaugurated for sports racing cars), they were successful in every round. At Le Mans Phil Hill and Olivier Gendebien recorded the last victory for a front-engined Ferrari in the 24 Hour classic, their third joint victory. The now legendary 250GTO racked up numerous prestigious victories worldwide in the GT category, to give Ferrari the Constructors' title.

During 1963 the 250GTO continued to dominate the GT category, once again giving Ferrari the Manufacturers' title. The Speed and Endurance World Challenge also fell to Ferrari, and included a fourth consecutive victory at Le Mans. In Formula One John Surtees, the British multiple motorcycling World Champion, was in the driving squad, and he proved equally adept on four wheels as on two, taking Ferrari's only F1 victory in the German Grand Prix at the Nurburgring, in a year that was dominated by Jim Clark and his Lotus 25-Climax. The 1964 Formula One season was a closely fought three-way battle between the Ferrari of John Surtees, the BRM of Graham Hill and the Lotus of Jim Clark – and it was not resolved until the last lap of the last race of the season, the Mexican Grand Prix. After championship leader Graham Hill had been involved in a collision, Jim Clark was leading the race comfortably, apparently cruising to his second title, when his engine failed on the final lap. Lorenzo Bandini, John Surtees' team-mate, generously allowed his team leader past to finish in second place. This was enough to secure the Drivers' Championship for John Surtees, and the Constructors' title for Ferrari. To this day he remains the only man to have won World Championships on both two and four wheels. In the

renamed International Championship for Makes Ferrari swept the board with the 250GTO, 250/275LM and P models, winning every round except for the Targa Florio, where victory went to Porsche.

In 1965, the last year of the 1.5-litre engine capacity in Formula One, Ferrari struggled, with two second places being the best that the team could muster, in a year where Jim Clark was again dominant in his Lotus to take the Drivers' Championship. In the sports and GT categories there was strong opposition from Ford, with the GT40 and Ford-powered AC Cobras. The 250GTO was no longer competitive against the much larger-engined AC Cobras, and because of the homologation difficulties experienced in 1964 with its intended replacement, the mid-engined 250/275LM, and then further problems in getting the 275GTB homologated, Ferrari announced that they would not contest the GT category. After prolonged negotiations the situation was resolved, and Ferrari joined the fray in mid-season, too late to mount an effective campaign. However, for the most part the sports prototypes still had the legs on the opposition, and took the International Championship for Makes, including a sixth successive Le Mans 24 Hour Race victory. This was to be the last Ferrari victory in this race, although it was not the marque's last appearance there.

The first year of the new 3-litre engine capacity Formula One in 1966 should have been a good one for Ferrari, as they were better prepared than many other teams at the start of the season. John Surtees won the second race of the season in Belgium, but it was Jack Brabham's Brabham Repco that dominated the season. Political intrigue and manoeuvrings at Ferrari saw John Surtees depart for Cooper-Maserati in mid-season, and apart from a 1–2 victory in their home grand prix at Monza, Ferrari were rarely in the hunt for the top places. In the sports car category Ford had really sorted out the GT 40 and were now the team to beat, which Ferrari only managed on two occasions, and thus had to be content with the runner-up slot in the championship.

The 1967 Formula One season was a bad one for Ferrari. Not once did their car pass the chequered flag in first place, but worse than that, they lost their rising star, Italian driver Lorenzo Bandini, who died in a fiery accident in the Monaco Grand Prix. The International Championship for Makes brought some consolation, as the season started with a commanding 1–2–3 victory in the Daytona 24 Hour Race – on Ford's home territory – with a pair of 330P4s and a 412P, arguably the most beautiful sports racing cars of all time. Although there was only one further victory at Monza, Ferrari took the championship from Porsche, who were becoming increasingly strong in the category.

In 1968 commercial sponsorship arrived in Formula One in a big way. The works Lotus 49s appeared in the red, white and gold livery of Gold Leaf cigarettes, to become Gold Leaf Team Lotus. Today corporate colours are an integral part of the multi-hued Formula One grid, but initially the concept was thought distasteful by many who felt that cars should race in their national colours. 1968 was also the year that aerodynamic wings first appeared on Formula One cars to increase downforce; they have become increasingly sophisticated over the years, as the science of aerodynamics has become better understood by the designers.

The final two years of the decade yielded only one Grand Prix victory for Ferrari, when the young Belgian Jacky Ickx won the 1968 French Grand Prix, his first victory in Formula One. Ferrari sports cars raced mainly in the hands of private entrants, but with little in the way of success in major races. Outnumbered by an armada of the hugely successful Porsche 908/2 model, the works 312P sports racing model contested the 1969 season, but second places in the Sebring 12 Hour Race and Spa 1000km were the best results of the season. However, there was some consolation on the sports racing side from the dominance of Peter Schetty's 212E 'Montagna' in the European Mountain Championship, in which he won every round he contested to take the title.

Another area where Ferrari did taste success was in the 1969 Tasman Championship, which was won for them by Chris Amon in a Tasman Dino. This late season series in the southern hemisphere was contested by many of the leading F1 drivers, and gained wide coverage in the European motoring press during the winter months. The wins in this series must have been a great morale booster for Ferrari, as they were the only major international victories of the year. 1969 also witnessed the purchase of 40 per cent of Ferrari by Fiat, and with a sizeable cash injection into the company, the future looked bright.

The 1960 model 250GT berlinetta was built on a 2400mm wheelbase (200mm shorter than the earlier models in the series). Consequently the 1956–9 examples are referred to as 'long wheelbase' ('LWB') and the 1960–3 models as 'short wheelbase' ('SWB'). The engine was a further development of the 3-litre V12 unit of the preceding model. Early cars in the series had no wing exhaust air vents or sleeves to the brake-cooling ducts in the front apron, but many subsequently had these features added. The 1960 series cars can be identified by the pronounced downward curve at the top rear of the door glass, and the location of the fuel filler in the top-left corner of the boot lid. This is an example of the early series, chassis number 1773GT, photographed at the Bridgehampton circuit in 1960.

The 250TR 59/60 is very similar in appearance to the 1959 model, because three of the 1959 cars were upgraded to 1960 specification to compete in that season. Ferrari also produced two additional cars, featuring independent rear suspension, which were of virtually identical appearance. This is the 1960 Le Mans winning car, chassis number 0774TR, which was driven to victory by Frere/Gendebien. (For this race it actually carried chassis number 0772TR, presumably to match up with travel carnet details, as 0772TR had been badly damaged in an accident in the Targa Florio the previous month.)

During 1959 Ferrari produced a V6-engined Dino 196S sports racing model, which was developed into the Dino 246S for 1960. These cars were almost identical in appearance to their V12 Testa Rossa stablemates, and the easiest way to identify them is by the number of intake trumpets under the perspex bonnet air intake – there are six on the Dino and twelve on the Testa Rossa. This is the Dino 246S of Hugus/Connell at Sebring in 1961.

(Opposite top) For the 1961 Formula One season the regulations changed, permitting only normally aspirated engines of a maximum capacity of 1.5 litres. Ferrari introduced their mid-engined 156 F1 model as their combatant for the season. It was fitted with a 1500cc twin overhead camshaft per bank V6 engine, of either 65 or 120 degree angle configuration. In this car Giancarlo Baghetti won the 1961 French Grand Prix on his World Championship race debut – a remarkable achievement that has never been equalled. On a more sombre note, it was also the car in which Wolfgang von Trips died in the Italian Grand Prix at Monza, with team-mate Phil Hill going on to win and becoming the first American World Champion. The 156 is seen here driven by Richie Ginther in the 1961 Dutch Grand Prix, which was won by von Trips in a similar car. The 156 continued to race in the 1962 season, but by then the competition had surpassed it, and it did not score a single victory in the World Championship series. During the 1962 season the 'nostril' nose was changed to a more conventional oval radiator intake. This was the last Ferrari F1 car to be fitted with wire wheels.

(Opposite bottom) For the 1961 season Ferrari's contender for GT honours, the 250GT SWB berlinetta, was provided with a lighter and stiffer chassis frame for the competition versions. Visually they can be identified by the straighter line to the top of the door glass, which had a quarter-light in the leading edge, and by the relocation of the fuel filler to the left rear wing. This is Stirling Moss drifting the Rob Walker-owned car, chassis number 2735GT, to victory in the Peco Trophy race at Brands Hatch in August 1961.

The principal sports racing model for the 1961 season was the 250TRI/61 with its 3-litre V12 engine, backed up by the similarly bodied but mid-engined Dino 246SP model with its 2.4-litre V6 engine. One of the most striking features of these cars was the 'nostril' or 'shark nose' bodywork that also featured on the 156 F1 cars. This is a 250TRI/61, with a 246SP in the background, pictured at Le Mans in 1961. The sister 250TRI/61 of Gendebien/Frere won the Le Mans race, while a Dino 246SP won the Targa Florio earlier in the year.

Pininfarina produced this variant on the 250GT berlinetta theme, which they called the 'Speciale Le Mans', on chassis number 2643GT for the 1961 Le Mans race where it retired. It fared better in its next outing at Daytona in 1962, where Stirling Moss drove it to victory in the GT category and fourth place overall.

The 250GTO was the ultimate development of the 250GT series and it continued the winning ways of its predecessors. It was built on a lightweight version of the 2400mm wheelbase chassis used on the preceding 250GT SWB berlinetta, and the engine was virtually up to full 250 Testa Rossa specification, with many lightweight components and a bank of six twin-choke carburettors to produce close to 300bhp. It was first presented at the Ferrari press conference in 1962, and won the GT category in its first race at Sebring a few weeks later. Here Innes Ireland in chassis number 3505GT leads Roy Salvadori in chassis number 3729GT into Druids Hill bend at Brands Hatch in August 1962.

During 1962 Ferrari produced a range of Dino SP models developed from the 246SP model of 1961. These were all mid-engined and had very similar bodywork, making identification at a glance very difficult. They included the 196SP, with a 1.98-litre V6 engine; the 246SP, which continued with a 2.4-litre V6 engine; the 248SP, with a 2.4-litre V8 engine; the 268SP, with a 2.6-litre V8 engine; and the 286SP with a 2.8-litre V6 engine. Not all the variants were in use at any one time, and engine types were swapped between cars. This is Ricardo Rodriguez in chassis number 0798, fitted with a V8 engine for the 1962 Le Mans test days.

Such was the prestige of victory at Le Mans that Ferrari built their last front-engined sports racing car specifically for the 1962 race. This was the 4-litre V12 type 330TRI/LM, chassis number 0808, which also featured the 'nostril' nose layout. In the hands of Phil Hill and Olivier Gendebien it gave Ferrari their third consecutive Le Mans win.

After Enzo Ferrari had refused to supply the 250GTO that he had on order, Count Volpi built his own car to a design by Giotto Bizzarrini. The result was the 250GT 'bread van' body. This offers an interesting study of a privately developed competition Ferrari of the period. It was produced on 250GT SWB chassis number 2819GT during 1962, with the engine lowered and moved rearwards to reduce the frontal area. This view shows how it earned its nickname!

The 1963 156 F1 car was a development of the preceding model, and late in the season the tubular chassis was replaced by a semi-monocoque unit. Despite the technical advances made by Ferrari, the car scored only one 1963 World Championship win. This is John Surtees on his way to that victory in the German Grand Prix at the Nurburgring.

During 1963 the 250GTO continued to be the car to beat in the GT category, going on to take the Manufacturers' title for the second consecutive year. This is chassis number 4399GT being driven by Graham Hill at Brands Hatch in the Guards Trophy race.

Ferrari had developed 4-litre versions of the GTO in 1962, and for 1963 they produced the 4-litre 330LM berlinetta specifically with the Le Mans race in mind. This is chassis number 4725SA driven by Lorenzo Bandini being harried by Tommy Hitchcock's 250GTO at Brands Hatch in August 1963, this car's only other race outing..

The 250P model was the sports racing car that Ferrari produced to contest the prototype class in 1963. It was their first attempt at a mid-engined sports racing car, and was powered by a derivative of the successful 3-litre V12 engine used in the hugely successful GT cars. A 4-litre engine was also tested in the model with a view to racing the following season. The 250P won three of the four rounds of the series, including Le Mans, where chassis number 0814 (seen here) was driven to victory by Scarfiotti/Bandini. This gave Ferrari their fourth consecutive victory in the race.

For the 1964 F1 season Ferrari employed a full monocoque chassis for the first time, in a car that could be adapted to use either a V8 or a flat-twelve engine, both of 1.5-litre capacity, which had been developed for use that year. The 158 and 1512 were the first Ferraris to wear the five-spoke magnesium alloy wheel, which has subsequently become a tradition of the marque in various guises. This is John Surtees in the 158 at the 1964 British Grand Prix at Brands Hatch, where he finished third. He went on to win the Drivers' Championship, becoming the first man to win World Championships on both two and four wheels, while Ferrari took the Constructors' title.

The 1500cc flat-twelve engine of the 1512 variant, with four coils and two rows of gleaming injection trumpets clearly visible.

For 1964 the 250GTO entered its third competitive season in the GT category, going on to take the honours and make it a hat-trick of titles. A new body style was provided from the pen of Pininfarina; it closely resembled the mid-engined 250LM – not without good reason, as Ferrari wanted to homologate the latter as a development of (and successor to) the GTO. As well as the three cars built with the new style body during 1964, four earlier models were rebodied to the new design. One of these was chassis number 4399GT of Maranello Concessionaires, seen here in 1964 at Brands Hatch being drifted by Innes Ireland.

(Opposite top) The 250LM was the first mid-engined Ferrari GT car – or at least it would have been if they had been able to homologate it successfully. In theory it was supposed to have been a development of the front-engined 250GT series, but it was more a 250P with a roof added. In fact only the first example had a 3-litre engine, all subsequent cars being fitted with 3.3-litre type 275 unit. The Automobile Club of Italy eventually gave it clearance in November 1964, prior to which it had to race in the prototype class. A privately entered 250(275)LM gave Ferrari their final Le Mans victory to date in 1965. This is the ex-Maranello Concessionaires example, chassis number 5907, beautifully restored to its original configuration.

(Opposite bottom) Ferrari developed another GT car for competition use during 1964. Based on the 275GTB road car, this was probably produced as a fall-back owing to the problems in registering the 250LM with the governing body. They encountered further problems getting the 275GTB homologated in 1965, and only after prolonged negotiations did it happen in the middle of the year, by which time any championship hopes were long gone. This is 275GTB 'Speciale' chassis number 06701, which was produced at the end of 1964. A similar car won the GT class at Le Mans in 1965.

For the 1964 season the sports prototype 250P was developed into the visually very similar 275P and 330P models. The new cars were slightly longer and lower, with different screen, roll hoop and rear lid details. They continued the success enjoyed by the 250P, with the 275P of Guichet/Vaccarella taking Ferrari's fifth successive victory at Le Mans in 1964. Entered by Maranello Concessionaires, the 330P, chassis number 0818, finished second, driven by Graham Hill/Jo Bonnier. It is seen here later in the year at Brands Hatch driven by Graham Hill.

The 1964 season was a very successful one, with wins in all the championships they entered, but 1965 was a relatively lean year for Ferrari. In F1 they fielded updated 158 and 1512 models, but a number of second and third places were the best that the team could muster. This is John Surtees in a 158 model at the Race of Champions at Brands Hatch in 1965.

A small series of 275GTB models were built in 1965 for privateer use in competition. These featured aluminium bodies (and sometimes special body details, like the inbuilt rectangular driving lights of this example, chassis number 07437), but were otherwise almost identical in appearance to the standard road model.

The Dino name was resurrected in 1965 with the introduction of the Dino 166P, powered by a 1.6-litre V6 engine. This was subsequently developed into the 2-litre 206P and S models. The original 166 had a domed roof, but was fitted with a 2-litre engine and then cut down to a 'Montagna' spider, with which Ludovico Scarfiotti won the 1965 European Mountain Championship. This is a 206S, chassis number 018, with similarly styled bodywork.

The larger-capacity sports prototype models for 1965 were the P2 series with a choice of engine sizes but similar body styles in either open or closed form. They were fitted with either 3.3-litre, 4-litre, or 4.4-litre V12 engines and were known as the 275P2, 330P2 and 365P respectively. This is the 365P, chassis number 0838, wearing the NART livery in which it raced at Le Mans in 1965. Aided by the 250LM privateer victories at Spa and Le Mans, Ferrari won the 1965 International Championship for Makes.

For 1966 the F1 regulations changed, with an increase in the permitted engine size to 3000cc, for which Ferrari produced the 312 model. The engine was developed from the 275 sports racing unit, but with a reduced stroke to bring the capacity within the 3-litre limit. On paper Ferrari seemed to be the best-prepared team for the new regulations, and they were favourites to win the championship. But it was not to be, as internal politics forced out their lead driver, John Surtees. With only two victories during the season, Ferrari finished runners-up in the Constructors' title to Brabham. The 312 was supplemented by a V6-engined variant with a 2.4-litre Dino engine called the 246. A gain in engine power was achieved for the 1967 season and fibreglass was used for the body panels, but it was visually similar to the 1966 version. From the Italian Grand Prix onwards the engines featured four-valve-per-cylinder heads. This is Chris Amon in the 1967 British Grand Prix at Silverstone, where he finished third.

(Opposite top) For the GT category the 275GTB of 1965 was updated with a longer nose for greater high-speed stability, and a competition derivative, the 275GTB/C, was available to private entrants. As with the earlier competition derivatives, this had a full aluminium body in thin gauge material, but whereas the 1965 competition cars had had a six twin-choke carburettor assembly, the 1966 cars had a triple arrangement with special curved and siamesed intake trumpets. This is chassis number 09035, which was driven by Pike/Piers Courage to eighth place overall and to GT class victory at Le Mans in 1966.

(Opposite bottom) The 206S model replaced the 206P for the 1966 season and was used in the small sports prototype class and in the European Mountain Championship. It had either a spider body featuring a prominent roll hoop or the closed coupé body shown here, and carried a specific Dino series of even chassis numbers.

John Surtees in the 312 F1 on his way to second place in the 1966 Daily Express International Trophy at Silverstone.

In the larger-capacity sports prototype class there were three groups of Ferrari contenders. The first of these was the 365P spider with its 4.4-litre V12 engine. It was similar to the 365P of 1965 but with minor mechanical changes and revisions to the body. Three were built and sold to private clients. This is David Piper in his example, chassis number 0836, at Snetterton in April 1966.

The second group consisted of the 365P2 models based on the previous year's 365P, which were upgraded for Maranello Concessionaires and NART. This is the former's example, chassis number 0826.

The works-entered cars were the strikingly beautiful 330P3 models, which were raced in both open and closed form. They were fitted with a 4-litre twin overhead camshaft per bank V12 engine. The first sports racing Ferrari to be fitted with fuel injection, it produced a claimed 420bhp. At the end of the season these cars were redesignated 412Ps and were sold to concessionaire teams to race in 1967. Chassis number 0844 was later rebodied as a CanAm spider, as seen above, but has recently been returned to its original configuration as shown below.

The 330P3 was developed into arguably the most beautiful Ferrari sports racing car ever made, the magnificent 330P4 model of 1967. It is visually very similar to its predecessor, and the harmony of line from any angle, coupled with the swooping curves, sculpted intakes, slots and neat rows of rivets make it a joy to behold, whether in open or closed form. This is Ludovico Scarfiotti in one of the works entries during the BOAC 500 at Brands Hatch in 1967.

At Le Mans in 1967 Ford gained revenge for Ferrari's crushing 1–2–3 victory at Daytona earlier in the year when the 330P4 was beaten into second place by the powerful Ford Mark IV – with an engine 3 litres larger than the Ferrari's. Nevertheless, the Manufacturers' title for 1967 still went to Ferrari. This 330P4 is one of the victorious Daytona trio, chassis number 0856.

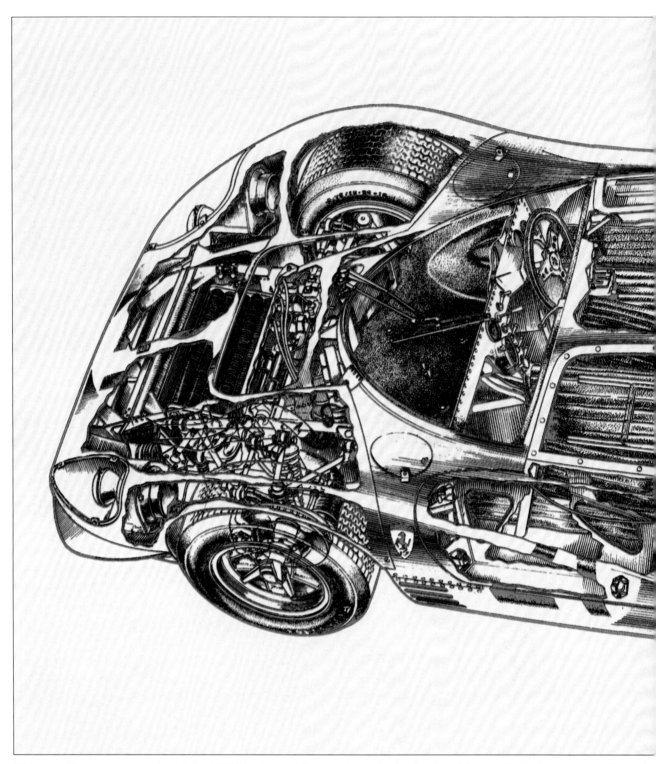

This magnificent cut-away view of the 330P4 by James Allington shows the intricacies of the mechanical components beneath the beautiful aluminium bodywork.

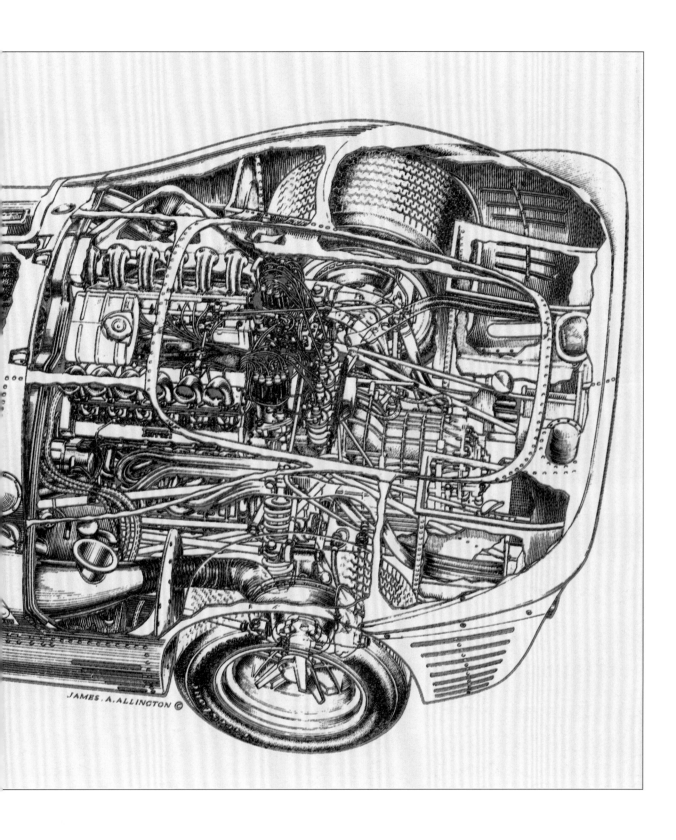

JAMES. A. ALLINGTON ©

The 330P4's beauty was not just skin deep, as shown by these views of the engine bay and rear end of chassis number 0856.

In 1968 aerodynamic appendages were introduced to F1 cars, and they started to sprout tabs and wings to increase downforce, thus improving roadholding. The 312 model was further developed for this season, but in the early races it was devoid of appendages and still very similar in appearance to the previous year's car, as can be seen in this view of Andrea de Adamich in the Race of Champions at Brands Hatch.

This view shows the engine complex and the inside vee 'spaghetti' exhaust system on Chris Amon's 312.

The engine bay of a Dino 206S. This example featured fuel injection, although carburettors were also used.

(Opposite top) During 1968 the Dino 206S continued to be competitive in the 2-litre sports prototype class in the hands of private entrants like Tony Dean, seen here at Brands Hatch during the BOAC 500 race.

(Opposite bottom) During 1967 a Dino 166 F2 car was built but made only one inauspicious race appearance. The car was refined and became the 246 Tasman and 166 F2 models for 1968. Like the F1 cars they were originally devoid of aerodynamic appendages, but had gained tabs and wings before the season ended. These are the two cars that made up Chris Amon's championship-winning 1969 Tasman campaign, seen on their trailer at the Levin circuit in New Zealand.

PPH 172666 L

Ferrari took a sabbatical from sports car racing in 1968 but they did prepare a car, chassis number 0866, for the American CanAm series. Called the 612 CanAm, it only appeared for the last round, but it retired after thick dust and debris from somebody else's accident blocked the fuel injection system. It reappeared for the 1969 series, with the revised bodywork shown here, and was competitive although it failed to win a race.

This is the 1969 312 F1 driven by Chris Amon at Monaco. Note the hydraulically adjustable rear aerofoil. This design was common at the time but was later banned after both Lotus 49s crashed out of the Spanish Grand Prix when their 'wings' collapsed. This picture was taken in the first practice session before the ban took effect. For the race, the car had only a small curved deflector plate atop the engine.

Ferrari returned to the sports car arena in 1969 with the works 312P model. This had a 3-litre V12 engine, in accordance with the current regulations, and ran in both coupé and spider configurations. It was an extremely low, smooth and elegant car, but with generally only a single car entry against an armada of works Porsche 908/2s the best it achieved was a couple of second places. The closed version is pictured at Le Mans in 1969, and the open version in the hands of Chris Amon at Brands Hatch in the BOAC 6 Hour Race the same year, where he finished fourth with Pedro Rodriguez.

Ferrari produced a single special car, bearing chassis number 0862, to contest the 1969 European Mountain Championship. Known as the 212E Montagna, it was basically a Dino 206S chassis fitted with a 2-litre flat-twelve engine based on the 1964/5 F1 unit, and with it Peter Schetty won the series.

Chapter 3

THE 1970s

The 1970 F1 car was a completely new design called the 312B, with a new flat-twelve engine of 3-litre capacity based on the design used for the 212E Montagna in 1969. It was fitted with twin overhead camshafts per bank, four-valve-per-cylinder heads and fuel injection to produce a claimed 450bhp. This is Jacky Ickx during the Monaco Grand Prix, in which he later retired. He went on to take three victories during the season, with both him and Ferrari finishing in the runner-up position in the respective championships.

Until his fatal crash during practice for the Italian Grand Prix, the 1970 Formula One season was dominated by Jochen Rindt's Lotus 72, but such had been his domination that he became the sport's only posthumous World Champion. The Ferrari challenge came together towards the end of the season, winning four of the last five races. Jacky Ickx won three, while in Italy his team-mate Clay Regazzoni gained his first grand prix victory. This gave Ferrari the runner-up spot in the Constructors' Championship, and Ickx and Regazzoni 2nd and 3rd places respectively in the Drivers' title. Graeme Lawrence gave Ferrari a second consecutive Tasman title, and also won the New Zealand Gold Star Series.

Ferrari had been expected to offer a strong challenge in 1971 after their strong finish in the previous season. They started well with a win by Mario Andretti in South Africa, but the new Tyrrell, with Jackie Stewart at the wheel, proved to be a very rapid combination, and convincingly took both Drivers' and Constructors' titles. The only other Ferrari victory came in the Dutch Grand Prix, courtesy of Jacky Ickx. This was the year that slick tyres were first used, and airboxes were fitted to increase the pressure of the air entering the induction system.

In sports car racing the years 1970 and 1971 saw the 'Battle of the Giants'. Group 5 sports cars had to be built in a minimum series of twenty-five cars, with an engine capacity not exceeding 5 litres. Porsche produced the the 917 model, with an air-cooled flat-twelve engine, which Ferrari countered with their V12-engined 512 model. Throughout both seasons Porsche nearly always had the upper hand, particularly in 1971 when the Ferraris were in the hands of privateers. The only 512 victory came in its second race in the 1970 Sebring 12 Hours, although there were subsequently many good placings, usually behind a 917.

Ferrari had little to show for their 1972 Formula One campaign, apart from a 1–2 win in the German Grand Prix, a couple of second places and some minor placings. It was the year of Emerson Fittipaldi and the Lotus 72D, who battled with Jackie Stewart in the Tyrrell 003 to become the world's youngest Formula One Champion at the age of twenty-five. However, if Ferrari didn't excel in Formula One during 1972, the World Championship for Makes was a very different matter. With a strong driver line-up, the 312PBs swept the board in all but one race, the Le Mans 24 Hours, which went to Matra. In every other round they took victory, and also filled the runner-up slot (except in the Monza 1000km and the Targa Florio), to take the Championship by a comprehensive margin from Alfa Romeo.

1973 was another barren year for Ferrari in Formula One, with only three fourth places and a few other minor placings to show for their efforts. In the sports car arena Matra were now the dominant force, eclipsing the 312PBs which scored only two 1–2 victories at Monza and the Nurburgring, although they frequently chased the Matras home. This gave Ferrari a higher tally of championship points at the end of the season, but as only the best seven results were counted, Matra took the title. Ferrari subsequently withdrew from all forms of racing apart from Formula One, in order to concentrate their efforts. From then on, sports racing and GT category efforts would be by private entrants only.

During 1973 Ferrari had noticed the performances of the young Austrian driver Niki Lauda in a largely uncompetitive BRM, and signed him to drive for Ferrari in 1974. In his first race for his new team in Argentina, he finished second, ahead of team-mate Clay Regazzoni. In the fourth race of the season he took his first victory for the team, leading Regazzoni home in the Spanish Grand Prix. There were further Ferrari victories in Holland with Lauda again beating Regazzoni, who won in Germany. Niki Lauda took nine pole positions in the fifteen races, and was frequently the fastest driver in the race, but unreliability – often when he was in the lead – cost him and Ferrari the respective titles.

For the 1975 season Niki Lauda again led the Ferrari challenge, ably backed up by Clay Regazzoni. In the early races of the season they still had the 312 B3 model, which was unable to match the pace of the competition, but once the new 312T (so-called because of the transverse gearbox layout) came on stream, Niki Lauda was the man to beat. Five victories gave him the Drivers' title, and with another win for team-mate Regazzoni in the Italian Grand Prix, the Constructors' title went to Ferrari for the first time since 1964.

The 1976 season started well for the Lauda/Ferrari combination, with victories in six of the first nine races, and they were leading the title race handsomely going into the tenth round at the Nurburgring in Germany. However, on the second lap of the German Grand Prix Lauda crashed heavily, and his car burst into flames. Thanks to the swift action of other drivers, he was extricated from the inferno; badly burned, he was given the last rites. But he survived, and miraculously he took part in the Italian Grand Prix five weeks later, where he finished fourth despite being in great pain. In spite of missing three races, including the one in which the accident occurred, he was still leading the title chase going into the final round in Japan, with only James Hunt in a position to challenge for the crown. In rain-soaked misty conditions, Niki Lauda withdrew from the race, considering the conditions too dangerous to continue, while James Hunt finished third to take the Drivers' title. Ferrari took the Constructors' title.

There were murmurs in some quarters that Niki Lauda had lost his nerve, so he had a point to prove in 1977, and also had a new team-mate in Carlos Reutemann. This was also the year that Renault introduced the 1.5-litre turbocharged engine to Grand Prix racing, an event that was to change the face of Formula One over the coming years, as would the ground-effect technology introduced on the Lotus 78 that season. Niki Lauda won three races during the season; together with a string of second and third places this gave him the Drivers' title for a second time, and also made him Ferrari's most successful Formula One driver of all time in terms of the number of wins, which now totalled fifteen. This was despite missing the final two races of the season because of political problems within the team which resulted in his chief mechanic, Ermano Cuoghi, being sacked. This was the final straw for Lauda and he walked out in disgust. His place for the final two races was taken by the young Canadian Gilles Villeneuve, whose name has become part of Ferrari folklore.

The 1978 season was dominated by the black and gold JPS-liveried Lotus 79, with which Mario Andretti took the Drivers' title. He was ably backed by his team-mate Ronnie Peterson, who lost his life after an accident in the Italian Grand Prix. Carlos Reutemann provided Ferrari with four victories, while team-mate Gilles Villeneuve won his home grand prix in Canada. This gave Ferrari the runner-up spot to Lotus in the Constructors' Championship.

In 1979 Reutemann moved to Lotus and South African Jody Scheckter joined Gilles Villeneuve at Ferrari to drive the 312T4. They proved to be a great combination and worked very well together. Gilles was probably the quickest, and certainly the most spectacular, driver over a single lap, but Jody's more conservative approach preserved the car better and reaped greater reward in terms of race results. However, Villenueve's flamboyant and exciting driving style won him a special place in the hearts of Ferrari enthusiasts the world over. They finished the season in fine style, with Scheckter taking the Drivers' title by four points from Villeneuve, with three victories each giving Ferrari the Constructors' title. It was a rewarding end to a decade that saw Ferrari win the Constructors' title four times, and their drivers take the Drivers' Championship three times.

One of the Dino 246 Tasman cars used by Chris Amon in 1969 was bought by Graeme Lawrence to compete in the 1970 Tasman series, which he did to good effect with a series victory. This is the sister car, chassis number 0010, used by Derek Bell in the 1969 series.

The 512S model was Ferrari's response to the Porsche 917 and was developed during 1969 to run in the Group 7 Sports Car category for the 1970 season. To comply with the current regulations Ferrari had to build a minimum of twenty-five examples, which they achieved ready for inspection by the FIA officials in January 1970. The motive power was a 5-litre fuel-injected V12 engine producing a claimed 550bhp. The model was run throughout the season both as a works car and by private entrants, in both coupé and spider forms. In performance terms they were fairly equally matched with their Porsche adversaries, but the German marque enjoyed greater reliability. The 512S took only one outright championship victory during the year, in the Sebring 12 Hour Race, although it did win the non-championship Fuji 200 Mile race in Japan, and an 'M' variant won the Kyalami 9 Hour Race. This is the coupé of Herbert Muller during the 1970 BOAC 1000km race at Brands Hatch.

Early in the 1971 F1 season Ferrari continued to use the previous year's 312 B, as they were still encountering problems with the derived 312 B2 model. It wasn't until the middle of the season that the 312 B was replaced by the 312 B2, which was then used throughout the remainder of the year and for the 1972 season. These pictures show Clay Regazzoni in the 1971 Race of Champions at Brands Hatch, which he won, and in the 1971 Monaco Grand Prix where he retired after a crash.

After privateer entries in the GT class with the 365GTB/4 'Daytona', the factory's 'Assistenza Clienti' department was given the go-ahead to build a series of five 365GTB/4C competition models in 1971. These had all-aluminium bodies and minimal trim, but they were relatively standard mechanically, apart from carefully balanced and put together engines. The cars were bought and raced by concessionaire and private teams and were updated during their competition careers, with wider arches and wheels plus some mechanical refinements. Two further series, of five cars each, were built in 1972 and 1973, and featured steel bodies. These had wider arches from new, and with commercial sponsorship of motor sport now in full swing they featured some colourful liveries, as can be seen from the two examples pictured.

For the 1971 season Ferrari offered 512S owners the more aerodynamic body panels that had first appeared on the winning car at Kyalami, and these upgraded models became known as the 512M models, the 'M' standing for *Modificato*. They were all coupé bodies, and featured a much more pronounced wedge shape than the 'S' body, as seen here on chassis number 1028 in its 1971 Le Mans livery, where it finished fourth. In 1971 they were only raced by private teams as the factory concentrated on its 3-litre sports prototype model.

(Opposite top) A CanAm car, the 712, was developed from 512 chassis number 1010, and was fitted with the largest-capacity engine ever produced by Ferrari: a 7-litre V12 unit, with four overhead camshafts per bank and fuel injection, producing a claimed 680bhp. It appeared once in 1971 as a works entry driven by Mario Andretti, who finished fourth at Watkins Glen, before being sold to NART to campaign for the 1972 season.

(Opposite bottom) A further development on the 512M theme was the Sunoco-sponsored car, chassis number 1040, which was produced by Roger Penske in the USA. This car was meticulously prepared and extremely quick, proving to be the fastest of all the Ferraris at Le Mans in 1971, but it didn't enjoy the best of luck. It is seen here at Spa Ferrari Days in 1996.

The 312P sports prototype for 1971 soon became known as the 312PB so that it could be more easily differentiated from the 1969 312P model. The 'B' suffix referred to the flat-twelve 'Boxer' engine layout. In effect a Formula One car with all-enveloping bodywork, it was both extremely quick and also very nimble, and it proved very competitive against the larger-engined 512Ms and Porsche 917s. It frequently led races through the 1971 season, but did not enjoy the best of luck, sometimes being sidelined by minor mechanical maladies but also getting entangled in other people's accidents. This is chassis number 0880, one of the cars campaigned by the factory during 1971.

(Opposite top) If 1971 had been a fraught learning year for the 312PB, then the trials and tribulations of that season bore fruit in 1972. Slight changes in the regulations meant that the cockpit profile changed and there were subtle changes to the overall shape. In mid-season they had to add body panels behind the rear wheels to meet a further change in regulations, and there were changes to wing, spoiler, tail length, and lighting layout depending on the circuit – long gone were the days when a car had a standard set-up whatever the circuit! The cars were almost totally dominant in the 1972 championship, missing only one victory in the eleven race series, which was at the prestigious Le Mans race. This is Peterson/Schenken's car, pictured in the BOAC 1000km at Brands Hatch, where it finished second to the sister car of Ickx/Andretti.

(Opposite bottom) Ferrari had used the 312 B2 for nearly two seasons when the 312 B3 was introduced in 1973. They tried various concepts for the new model, including this example which soon earned the nickname 'Spazzaneve' ('snowplough') for obvious reasons! It was only used in testing and never raced.

The 312 B3 underwent numerous changes during the season, with alterations being made to the body profile to try to extract reasonable performance. However, the drivers were fighting a losing battle against the competition, and the season's results were dismal. This is Jacky Ickx in the 1973 British Grand Prix at Silverstone, where he could do no better than eighth place.

Further developments of the 312PB sports prototype were made for the 1973 season, but the Matra Simca team took the title at the final round. At the end of the season Ferrari withdrew from all categories of motor sport as a works team apart from Formula One, in order to concentrate their energies in that direction. This is chassis number 0888, showing the revised body layout with a full width rear wing and snorkel injection air intakes frequently used during 1973.

This is chassis number 16363, an example of the final series of 365GTB/4C models constructed for the 1973 season, wearing another very colourful livery. This car was entered at Le Mans that year by the French Ferrari importer Charles Pozzi, taking victory in the GT class driven by Elford/Ballot Lena.

After a large amount of pre-season work and testing on the 312 B3 F1 car, and with the new driver line-up of Niki Lauda and the returning Clay Regazzoni, the F1 project came together under the guidance of Mauro Forghieri. Another key personality to arrive on the scene in this season was the young Luca di Montezemolo, a name once again heavily associated with Ferrari in more recent years. The body shape of the new car was a refinement of the version seen late in 1973, featuring a full width front wing and a tall vertical airbox above the engine. The cars proved competitive, with ten pole positions, three victories, and numerous podium finishes during the season. The Drivers' Championship was only lost in the very last race of the season to Emerson Fittipaldi in his McLaren. This is Niki Lauda in the 1974 British Grand Prix at Brands Hatch.

The 312 B3 was retained for the first two races of the 1975 season in South America, until the replacement 312T was introduced at the South African Grand Prix. The 'T' in the model designation referred to the new 'trasversale' (transverse) gearbox. At a glance the car was similar to the preceding model, but the nose was slimmer and it was generally more refined aerodynamically. The cylinder heads had been redesigned and power output was up to a claimed 500bhp. Its grand prix debut was disappointing, and the second race was a disaster: Lauda and Regazzoni collided on the first lap, after the former had been pushed into his team-mate by another driver. But things improved at Monaco, where Lauda gave Ferrari its first victory in the principality for twenty years. Niki Lauda went on to take a total of five grand prix wins during the season, and in the process gained the Championship titles for himself and Ferrari. This is Lauda in the non-championship International Trophy at Silverstone, which he also won.

(Opposite top) The 312T continued its winning ways at the start of the 1976 season, taking victories in the first three grand prix, two for Lauda and one for Regazzoni. The replacement 312T2 was introduced at the first of the European Grand Prix in Spain, where Niki Lauda finished second. He went on to win a further two races before his horrific accident in the German Grand Prix, and was still in with a chance of the title going into the final round in Japan. He withdrew from the race because of the appalling weather conditions, and consequently lost the title to James Hunt by a single point, although Ferrari won the Constructors' title. The 312T2 was visually different from its predecessor owing to regulation changes affecting the airbox design, which was replaced by the intake ducts on either side of the cockpit. This is Clay Regazzoni in the Belgian Grand Prix at Zolder, where he finished second to team-mate Niki Lauda.

(Opposite bottom) For 1977 the 312T2 F1 car continued in use, with an increase in power having been found over the winter months, plus revisions made to the body panels, resulting in smaller NACA air intakes on the cockpit sides. It was on this version of the 312T2 that the Fiat logo first appeared on a Ferrari grand prix car. On the driver front, Carlos Reutemann replaced Clay Regazzoni alongside Niki Lauda, and between them they took four grand prix wins, with Lauda regaining the Drivers' title, and Ferrari making it a hat-trick of consecutive successes in the Constructors' series.

By 1978 the understanding of aerodynamic considerations was becoming a major factor in the design of F1 cars, and the 312T3 reflected this increase in awareness, with a slimmer nose profile and a body shape designed around airflow patterns. It was also designed to use the new tubeless radial-ply tyres which Michelin brought into F1 for the 1978 season, soon to be followed by Goodyear. The power unit and gearbox had proved adequate in 1977, so there was little change there and the quoted power output was similar. Niki Lauda had left the team to go to Brabham, so Carlos Reutemann assumed the role of team leader, backed up by a young Canadian driver who in a very short time would become a Ferrari legend – Gilles Villeneuve. Reutemann took four wins during the season and Villeneuve won his home grand prix, but this was the year of the Lotus 79 in which Mario Andretti took both the Drivers' and Constructors' titles, aided by his team-mate Ronnie Peterson.

(Opposite top) In 1975 Luigi Chinetti's North American Racing Team had entered a fairly standard 365GT4/BB model developed from the road car in the Le Mans 24 Hour Race, although it did not participate owing to problems with another of his entries. This was subsequently developed with more radical and lighter body panels, wider wheels and a higher degree of engine tune, and raced at Le Mans in 1977 in the IMSA category, where it finished sixteenth overall. In 1978 it was joined by four 5-litre flat-twelve-engined 512BB derived versions, but it was the sole survivor of the Ferrari quintet at the end of the race. This is the sister NART-entered 512 BB, which was lying eleventh overall and second in the IMSA class when it retired just before three-quarter distance.

(Opposite bottom) For 1979 the concessionaires persuaded Ferrari to build a series of 512 BB/LM models at their 'Assistenza Clienti' department in Modena, specifically with the IMSA category at Le Mans in mind. They were raced elsewhere on occasion, usually on faster circuits that did not place too great a premium on handling. This was because they were developed from a road car with the gearbox below the engine, thus they had a relatively high centre of gravity that hindered their cornering speed. Four examples appeared at the 1979 Le Mans race, this being the NART-entered example during the race.

In 1979 Carlos Reutemann left the Ferrari F1 team and his place was taken by the South African driver Jody Scheckter, who joined Gilles Villeneuve to drive the 312T4 model. Lotus had proved the effectiveness of the ground-effect principle with the Lotus 79, and all the other manufacturers were obliged to follow suit to remain competitive. The 312T4 utilised this to good effect, and retained a slightly more powerful version of the flat-twelve engine that had given such good service since the beginning of the decade. Both drivers enjoyed three wins apiece during the season, although Scheckter's more regular placings gave him the Drivers' Championship, with Ferrari again taking the Constructors' title. It was during this season that Villeneuve really won the hearts of Ferrari enthusiasts, with tremendous displays of courage and daring that sometimes defied belief. One such incident was his wheel-banging duel with Rene Arnoux in the latter stages of the French Grand Prix at Dijon, when he snatched second place by just 0.15 of a second from Arnoux. This is Jody Scheckter in the T4 at the 1979 British Grand Prix at Silverstone.

Chapter 4

THE 1980S

The year 1980 proved to be a very lacklustre one for Ferrari in Formula One, and the new 312T5 model was far less competitive than its predecessor. The new model was a development of the T4 and was very similar to it in appearance, but the opposition had become stronger, particularly the Williams car which was the dominant force of the season, easily winning the Constructors' title, with Alan Jones taking the Drivers' title. This was the last flat-twelve-engined Ferrari F1 car, and they moved to a 1500cc V6 turbo unit at the end of the season. The 312T5 is seen here in the hands of Gilles Villeneuve in the 1980 British Grand Prix at Brands Hatch.

The first year of the new decade saw the emergence of Williams as a constructor to be reckoned with, after their cars had finished the latter part of the 1979 season strongly. Ferrari retained its championship-winning pairing from the previous year to drive the new 312T5 model. However, it was to prove a frustrating year for both of them, as the car was off the pace and the best either could do was a fifth place. After the triumph of 1979 this was a morale-crushing scenario, and Jody Scheckter announced his retirement from the sport at the end of the 1980 season.

For 1981 Villeneuve was joined by the Frenchman Didier Pironi to mount the Ferrari challenge in their first turbo-charged grand prix car, the 126 CK. Ferrari had learned the art of turbo technology quickly and had an extremely powerful engine; unfortunately the chassis dynamics were below par, and lacked the grip of its major competitors. Gilles Villeneuve scored two victories, one in Monaco and one in Spain. In the latter he won largely by racecraft, as he led a train of faster cars for lap after lap, and only 1.24 seconds covered the first five finishers.

The 126 CK was refined for 1982, becoming the 126 C2, and the same drivers were retained to lead the Ferrari challenge. The new car was an improvement over its predecessor, although it didn't taste victory until the Formula One Constructors' Association boycotted the San Marino Grand Prix. The result was a Ferrari 1–2, but Gilles Villeneuve was furious as he felt that Pironi had disobeyed team orders to take victory, when he had been trying to slow the pace to conserve fuel and ensure a Ferrari victory. The previously happy relationship became acrimonious, with Villeneuve refusing to speak to Pironi. It was under this cloud that the team went to the next grand prix at Zolder in Belgium, and it was here, near the end of the practice session, that Gilles Villeneuve had the horrific accident that took his life. Ferrari immediately withdrew from the race, and the team headed home, heartbroken at the loss of one of their best-loved drivers. Pironi continued with Ferrari's challenge alone until he was joined by fellow Frenchman Patrick Tambay at the Dutch Grand Prix. Pironi led the Drivers' Championship going into the twelfth round in Germany, where he too crashed heavily in practice, resulting in awful leg injuries that ended his F1 career. Of small consolation in light of the accident, Patrick Tambay took his first victory for Ferrari in the race, and Ferrari went on to win the 1982 Constructors' title. Keke Rosberg in the Williams only overhauled Pironi's points tally in the last race of the season to take the Drivers' Championship.

For 1983 Renault's Rene Arnoux joined Patrick Tambay at Ferrari and did very well, with three victories and numerous placings putting him in contention for the Drivers' title, but his chances came to nothing when he failed to score any points in the final two races of the season. Patrick Tambay dedicated his only win of the season, in the San Marino Grand Prix, to his friend Gilles Villeneuve, but his consistent placings helped Ferrari to take the Constructors' title once again.

In contrast, 1984 was a lean year for Ferrari in a season dominated by McLaren, with only one victory courtesy of new recruit Michele Alboreto in Belgium, although some good placings by both Alboreto and Arnoux gave Ferrari the runner-up spot in the Constructors' title race, albeit with fewer than half the points total amassed by McLaren, such was their dominance. They remained all-powerful through 1985, although Alboreto's wins in Canada and Germany and some good placings kept him in the title hunt for most of the season. He eventually finished second in the Drivers' Championship, with Ferrari once again taking the runner-up spot in the Constructors' title race. The 1986 season was a battle between McLaren and Williams, and Ferrari didn't record a single victory, although Alboreto and Johansson had a string of podium finishes between them. The 1987 season began with little promise, although results improved as the season progressed. New Ferrari recruit Gerhard Berger spun out while leading the Portugese Grand Prix, but recovered to finish second to Alain Prost's McLaren. Berger then won the last two races of the season in Japan and Australia, leading team-mate Michele Alboreto home to a Ferrari 1–2 in the latter, and giving the team some hope for the next season.

In 1988 Enzo Ferrari, the company's founder and its driving force, died on 14 August aged ninety and the motoring racing world mourned the loss of one of its best-known and longest-serving combatants, as driver, team manager and manufacturer. After over a decade, this year also saw turbochargers used on Formula One cars for the last time, the governing body having decided that only naturally aspirated engines of 3.5-litre capacity could be used from 1989 onwards. Ferrari's expectations after the last two races in 1987 came to nothing in a season again totally dominated by the McLarens of Alain Prost and Ayrton Senna. The only high spot of the season for Ferrari was a 1–2 victory in the Italian Grand Prix at Monza, which the drivers dedicated to their recently departed leader. It seemed a rather miraculous success, after Senna's leading McLaren crashed when lapping a back marker. The McLaren duo tied up the Drivers' title, with Gerhard Berger a distant third, and Ferrari were a distant runner-up in the Constructors' Championship.

The final year of the decade was approached by Ferrari enthusiasts with their usual irrepressible optimism, hoping that 1989 would be Ferrari's year. But it was to be denied yet again, as it was the seemingly invincible McLaren duo that tied up the series again, despite the hostility between the two drivers. Ferrari had recruited Nigel Mansell to replace Michele Alboreto, and the optimism of the fans was raised when he scored a debut win for Ferrari in the first race of the season in Brazil. He followed this with a victory in Hungary, while Gerhard Berger won in Portugal – but that was it in terms of outright wins, and thus came to an end a decade that had promised much but delivered little, except sadness, for Ferrari.

Ahead of the 1980 season the 512BB/LM had undergone further aerodynamic studies in the Pininfarina wind tunnel. These resulted in a change to the shape of the cooling intakes in the rear wings, together with a revision of the body base line between the wheel arches, which was deeper and flatter. A comparison of the differences can be made between the later 'European University'-liveried example, chassis number 32129 (above), and the earlier British-entered car, chassis number 27577 (below), looking somewhat scrappy late in the 1980 Le Mans race, after borrowing the rear body section from another car that had retired. Out of five examples that started the 1980 race, these were the only two to reach the finish, in tenth and twenty-third places respectively. In 1981 and 1982 a pair of 512 BB/LMs managed to make the finish on each occasion, the highest-placed examples coming fifth and sixth overall in the respective years.

The Carma FF was a private Ferrari-based racing car produced for the 1980 season by Carlo Facetti and Martino Finotto, the name being derived from their Christian names, and surname initials. This brutish 308 silhouette model, with a twin turbocharged V8 engine, was extremely powerful and fast, but it also proved to be rather fragile and was abandoned at the end of the season.

The first turbocharged Ferrari F1 car made its public debut in practice for the 1980 Italian Grand Prix, but was not raced until further development had taken place over the winter. It was initially known as either the 126 CK or 126 CX, depending which manufacturer's turbo units were used, but when it was decided to use only the KKK units the car became simply the 126 C. The twin turbo 1.5-litre engine produced a claimed 560bhp, but apart from the motive power the car's construction and layout were very similar to the preceding normally aspirated model. In 1981 Gilles Villeneuve had a new team-mate in Frenchman Didier Pironi, as Jody Scheckter had retired from the sport. The season didn't start well for the new package, owing to various problems, but Villeneuve managed two wins and both drivers got into the points occasionally. This is Villeneuve on his way to victory in the 1981 Monaco Grand Prix, his first of the season.

The Michelotto concern in Padova, who work closely with Ferrari on development projects, produced a series of Group 4 rally cars based on the 308GTB road model, which were very successful in private hands, particularly those of the Charles Pozzi team in France, during 1981 and 1982. These two views show the Pozzi car in the Pioneer livery that it wore during the 1982 season.

The 126 C laid bare as Didier Pironi waits for adjustments to be completed before continuing his practice session.

The Formula One car for the 1982 season was designated the 126 C2, for which the previous year's driver pairing of Villeneuve and Pironi were retained. Unfortunately, after the San Marino Grand Prix at Imola, a bitter dispute arose between the drivers. With some justification, Villeneuve believed that Pironi had robbed him of victory when they were running first and second by not holding station, but rather pushing the pace and passing him, thus risking both drivers running out of fuel at a circuit where consumption was critical. The acrimony boiled over into the practice session for the next race, where Villeneuve crashed fatally while trying to better his team-mate's time. Later in the season Pironi suffered a terrifying accident in practice for the German Grand Prix, which smashed his legs and ended his F1 career. Patrick Tambay and later Mario Andretti were drafted into the team, and Ferrari scored enough points to take the Constructors' title, in what had been a traumatic year. The sliding skirt ground-effect technology was banned for the following season, and the 126 C2 was developed into the interim 126 C2B model pictured here, which was used for the first half of the 1983 season.

(Opposite top) The 126 C3 F1 car was introduced mid-way through the 1983 season and was similar in appearance to the preceding 126 C2B (and to the succeeding 126 C4 model). Despite achieving only two overall victories during the 1983 season with the two models, Patrick Tambay and his new team-mate and compatriot Rene Arnoux managed to amass enough points between them to win the Constructors' title for Ferrari for the second successive year. For 1984 the 126 C4 was introduced, and Patrick Tambay was replaced by Michele Alboreto. Although still powered by a twin turbo V6 unit, the new car's engine was substantially redesigned and lightened, producing a claimed 660bhp. Although Michele Alboreto won the Belgian Grand Prix, and both drivers scored some reasonable placings, the season could not be judged a great success. This is Rene Arnoux during the 1984 British Grand Prix at Brands Hatch.

(Opposite bottom) The twin turbo 1.5-litre V6 engine of the 126 C4 model.

In 1983 not a single Ferrari had taken part in the Le Mans 24 Hour Race, but in 1984 the Bellancauto team entered a single 512 BB/LM. This was chassis number 35529, which had a much truncated and unique body style designed by Ing. Palanca and was sponsored by the Ferrarelle mineral water company, in an attractive 'bubble' livery. It retired at just after one-third distance. This was to be the last time that a Ferrari would race at Le Mans for a number of years.

(Opposite top) The 156/85 was the car on which Ferrari pinned their hopes for the 1985 season. It was essentially an upgraded C4, with the turbochargers moved from their position above the 1.5-litre V6 engine and relocated to either side of it; together with redesigned cylinder heads and other changes, this produced a claimed 780bhp in race trim. After the first race Rene Arnoux and Ferrari parted company, and the Swedish driver Stefan Johansson replaced him alongside Michele Alboreto. With two victories and a number of second places, Michele Alboreto was in contention for the Drivers' title until late in the season, but in the end both he and Ferrari finished as runners up in the respective championships. This is Stefan Johansson during the 1985 European Grand Prix at Brands Hatch.

(Opposite bottom) The 1986 Ferrari Formula One contender was designated the F1-86, and it was a further development of the twin turbo 1.5-litre V6 engine theme that the team had pursued since 1980. Visually it can be most easily identified from its predecessor by a return to the high engine cowl profile of the 126 C2B and C3. The car proved unreliable and posted numerous retirements, with the best result being second place for Alboreto in Austria, while Johansson recorded a quartet of third places during the season. This is Stefan Johansson in the 1986 British Grand Prix at Brands Hatch.

For the 1987 season the Ferrari contender was the F1-87 model, with Gerhard Berger joining Michele Alboreto in the driving squad. Visually the new model was a refined version of the F1-86, with a different profile to the side pods, owing to the relocation of the radiator, and a shallower cowl over the engine. The spate of retirements of the previous year continued almost until the end of the season, when Gerhard Berger scored back-to-back wins in the last two races on the F1 calendar, starting from pole position each time. Finishing the season on a high gave hope for 1988. The 1988 version was a mildly modified F1-87 called the F1 87/88C for the final year of the turbocharged era. This car was more reliable but there were still no victories in a year dominated by McLaren. Although Ferrari finished as runners-up in the Constructors' title, they had fewer than one-third of the points of the McLaren team. The F1-87 is seen here with Gerhard Berger at the wheel at Imola.

The 1989 F1 season was one of change for everyone, as the regulations banned the 1.5-litre turbocharged engine in favour of a 3.5-litre normally aspirated unit. Ferrari's answer was to employ the highly respected English designer John Barnard to produce the F1-89 or 640 model. This had a fuel-injected 3.5-litre V12 engine mated to a seven-speed longitudinal gearbox and produced a claimed 600bhp. This model featured the first semi-automatic gearbox in F1, a system that has since been highly developed, and is now *de rigueur* for all F1 cars. In plan the body was shaped like a Coke bottle, with a long and low anteater-style nose section. Nigel Mansell joined Gerhard Berger on the driving team, and to everybody's surprise gave the car a maiden victory in Brazil. The gearbox proved unreliable and resulted in numerous retirements, but despite this Mansell won again in Hungary and Gerhard Berger won in Portugal.

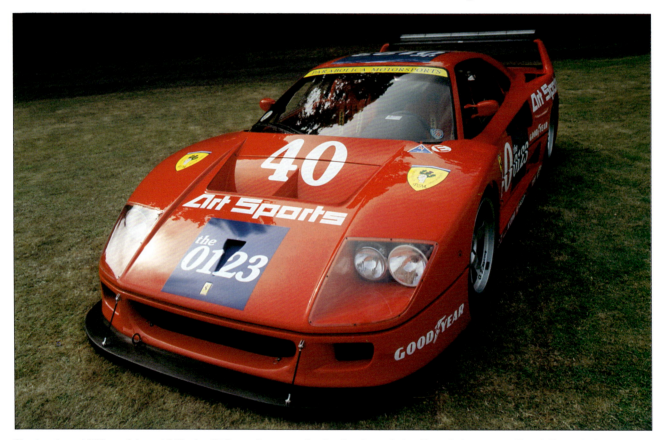

During late 1988 and into 1989 the F40 road car, at the instigation of the French importers Pozzi Ferrari France, was developed into a racing model to contest the IMSA series in the USA. The original road car had caused a sensation on its announcement in 1987, with its 'race car for the road' appeal and stunning appearance. The F40LM race version carried the concept to its logical conclusion. It raced in the series in late 1989 and throughout 1990, posting some good placings, and was driven by the likes of Jean-Pierre Jabouille and Jean Alesi. This is chassis number 88522, one of the small series produced.

Chapter 5

THE 1990s

For the 1990 season Ferrari recruited triple World Champion Alain Prost to partner Nigell Mansell in the 641 and 641/2 models. Alterations to the engine, including the provision of five-valve-per-cylinder heads, had increased the power output to a claimed 680bhp. It was visually very similar to the preceding model in overall shape, retaining the Coke bottle plan profile. The major differences were in the radiator outlets in the body sides, and the configuration of the engine cowl airbox, which was taller. Hopes were high for the championship with Prost in the team, and he almost delivered the goods with five wins which kept him in contention for the championship until the penultimate Grand Prix in Japan. Here he was pushed off the road by Ayrton Senna, who went on to take a hollow Drivers' title. Both Prost and Ferrari were runners-up in the respective titles.

The flame of optimism was rekindled when the Ferrari driver line-up for the 1990 season was announced, as three times World Champion Alain Prost came to join Nigel Mansell. It turned out to be one of Ferrari's more competitive seasons, with Alain Prost winning five races and Nigel Mansell one. Along with some good placings, this put Prost in line for his fourth Drivers' title, and Ferrari were in with a chance of the Constructors' Championship. However, the acrimony between Prost and his former McLaren team-mate Ayrton Senna came to a head in the Japanese Grand Prix, when the latter forced Prost off the road in a race where he needed to score points to maintain his challenge. Thus Senna took the Drivers' title, with Prost finishing as runner-up, and Ferrari came second in the Constructors' Championship.

In 1991 Nigel Mansell left Ferrari for Williams, and Jean Alesi joined Alain Prost to give the team an all-French driver line-up. But it proved to be a dismal year for the team with not a single victory, and only a string of reasonable placings to show for their efforts. Alain Prost became increasingly critical of the management of the team, and departed before the last race of the season, in which he was replaced by Gianni Morbidelli. Ayrton Senna took his third Drivers' title, but the sensation of the season was a young German driver's performance on his practice debut for the new Jordan team in the Belgian Grand Prix: everyone was talking about Michael Schumacher.

The 1992 Ferrari campaign was even more dismal than in the previous year, with Ivan Capelli joining Jean Alesi. The best results during the season were third places in the Spanish and Canadian Grand Prix.

Ivan Capelli never shone, and seemed to show a propensity for flying off the road, and he was replaced by Nicola Larini before the end of the season. The 1993 season continued in the doldrums, even with the more experienced driver pairing of Jean Alesi and Gerhard Berger, making a return to the team. Again there were no victories, and a second place in the Italian Grand Prix, plus a couple of third and fourth places and some minor placings, was the sum total for the season.

The 1994 driver pairing remained the same at Ferrari, and the new 412T1B seemed more competitive than its predecessor. After Ayrton Senna's fatal accident at Imola early in his first season at Williams, the main protagonists for the title were his team-mate Damon Hill and Michael Schumacher in the Benetton. The latter succeeded, after a controversial crash in the last race of the season in Australia, in becoming the first German to take the title. The Ferrari drivers enjoyed a number of good placings, and then at last, in the German Grand Prix, Gerhard Berger gave Ferrari their first victory since the 1990 season, on his way to third in the Drivers' Championship, with Ferrari finishing in the same position in the Constructors' Championship. It was also in 1994 that the 333SP sports prototype made its debut in the IMSA/WSC series in the USA, sweeping all before it and rekindling fond memories of the great sports racing Ferraris of yesteryear.

For the 1995 season the drivers remained the same for the third consecutive year, with Alesi and Berger again carrying the hopes of the fans on their shoulders. The maximum engine capacity was reduced to 3 litres, and Ferrari fielded the 412T2 model. The new model was competitive, but the championship title chase was once again between Hill (Williams) and Schumacher (Benetton) respectively. After several good placings in the early races, Jean Alesi scored his first grand prix win in Canada, and although there were further good results that remained the only Ferrari victory of the season. Michael Schumacher went on to take his second consecutive Drivers' title in the Benetton in dominant style. Across the Atlantic the 333SPs continued their winning ways in the IMSA/WSC series, and in Europe an F40LM, developed from the F40 road car, won a round of the BPR GT race series.

In 1996 it was all change at Ferrari, as the reigning double World Champion driver Michael Schumacher arrived amidst a blaze of publicity. Eddie Irvine was recruited from Jordan as his team-mate. They were to drive the new F310 model, powered by Ferrari's first V10 engine. In the early season races Michael Schumacher had a pair of second places and a third, before recording his first victory for the team in a spectacular drive in the pouring rain in the Spanish Grand Prix. The cars then went through a terrible period of unreliability problems in mid-season, but these were eventually overcome and Schumacher took back-to-back victories in the Belgian and Italian Grand Prix. With a third place in the Portuguese Grand Prix and a second in the final round in Japan, he finished third in the Drivers' Championship, with Ferrari second in the Constructors' title. Again the fans had to to be optimistic and think 'maybe next year', but three victories in the season was Ferrari's best effort since 1990. The 333SP sports racing car continued to be competitive in its third season, and would continue to be so through to the end of the decade. A further development of the F40,

the F40GT-E, won a round of the BPR GT race series.

In 1997 the development of the F310 model, designated the F310B, was not fully competitive in the early races, although there were some second and third places, but it all came good in a wet Monaco Grand Prix when Schumacher won, with his team-mate third. He followed this up with wins in Canada, France, Belgium and Japan, so that he was in contention to win the title going into the last race, the European Grand Prix in Portugal. He was leading the race when the controversial collision with his rival for the championship, Jacques Villeneuve, occurred, sending Schumacher into retirement, and handing the crown to Villeneuve. At least the seasonal victory tally was rising, but the top rewards were still just out of reach.

For 1998 the team remained the same, driving the F300 model. As in 1997, the season started with the cars off the pace of the front-running team, which was now McLaren. However, by the third race in Argentina there was something to smile about, as Michael Schumacher won, with Eddie Irvine third. The next three races all saw the drivers in podium positions, but they didn't win. At the next race in Canada, the result was a repeat of the one in Argentina, while the next round in France saw the first Ferrari 1–2 in a Grand Prix for eight years. In the next round at Silverstone the Argentine result was repeated again, despite Schumacher receiving a ten-second Stop-Go penalty, and actually finishing the race in the pit lane. The next two races were lacklustre for Ferrari, and then Michael Schumacher won again in Hungary. At Spa there was a highly publicised accident when Michael Schumacher ran into the back of a slowing David Coulthard, neatly removing his right front wheel. He drove back to the pits on three wheels to retire. At their home grand prix at Monza there was another Ferrari 1–2, while a second place for Schumacher in the European Grand Prix at the Nurburgring meant that the title fight, this time between Schumacher and Hakkinen, was down to the last race again. Once again Ferrari were thwarted, as a hydraulic problem on the grid forced Schumacher to relinquish his pole position and start from the back of the grid. In the end he retired with a blown tyre, and team-mate Irvine finished second, so again the ultimate prize eluded them.

The driver line-up at Ferrari remained constant for the fourth consecutive year in 1999, now with the F399 model. In the opening round of the season in Australia Eddie Irvine took his first win for Ferrari – it was also the first grand prix victory of his career. Michael Schumacher finished second in Brazil, before winning the San Marino Grand Prix to equal Niki Lauda's record of fifteen Ferrari F1 victories. At the very next race in Monaco he broke the record, with Eddie Irvine finishing second, for an emotional post-race celebration. From this high point the season seemed to turn in McLaren's favour, with the biggest blow to any championship hopes occurring in the British Grand Prix, when Michael Schumacher broke his leg in a first lap accident. This put paid to his hopes in the Drivers' title battle, and seriously hindered Ferrari's chances for the Manufacturer's crown. Mika Salo was drafted in to back up Eddie Irvine, who was still in a position to take the Drivers' title, after his first race win and several solid placings during the season. He rose to the challenge of his new role as team leader, ably backed by Mika Salo,

taking victories in Austria and Germany. Michael Schumacher returned to the team for the penultimate race in Malaysia, to assist with Irvine's title challenge, and gave his team-mate the victory he needed to take the chase to the final round in Japan. With both the Drivers' and Constructors' titles at stake, once again everything hinged on the result of the final race, at a circuit where Ferrari and Irvine had traditionally performed well. Although Michael

Alain Prost stayed with the team for 1991 and was joined by Jean Alesi to race the 642 and 643 F1 cars. These were almost identical to their predecessors, but now produced a claimed 710bhp. Unfortunately it was an uphill struggle after the previous season, and unreliability blighted the drivers' efforts, with neither scoring a single victory. Alain Prost was vocally critical of the team, and did not take part in the last race of the season. This is the 643 model used from the seventh race of the season.

Schumacher claimed pole position, Irvine was not his usual brilliant best on the Suzuka circuit. Schumacher's second place in the race meant that after sixteen years Ferrari won the Constructors' Championship again, but with only third place Eddie Irvine was runner-up in the Drivers' title chase. Fans would have to wait for the next century to see whether a Ferrari driver could win that elusive crown.

(Opposite) In 1992 Jean Alesi was joined by Ivan Capelli to drive the F92A and later in the season the derivative F92AT F1 cars. Capelli never really got to grips with Formula One and had a number of accidents, while the reliability problems that had afflicted the 1991 car continued, and the best results that Jean Alesi could muster during the season were a couple of third places. The car itself is easy to identify from other Ferrari F1 cars of the period because of the elegant oval radiator air intakes in the side pods.

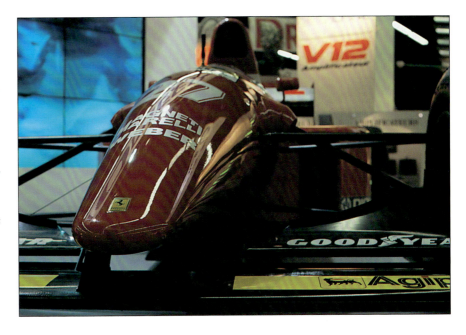

(Right) A close-up view of the penetrating nose cone of the F93A.

For the 1993 season Ferrari introduced the F93A F1 car, with Jean Alesi now partnered by the returning Gerhard Berger. The main visual feature of the car was the broad white band around its cockpit perimeter and air box, thus making it easy to identify among contemporary F1 Ferraris. Under the skin the V12 engine was coupled to a six-speed transverse gearbox, after four years with a longitudinal layout. It proved to be well up to the pace of its peers, although the Williams team was once again the dominant force. Alesi managed a second place in Italy after a third in Monaco, with Berger taking a third in Hungary, but otherwise the season was largely a catalogue of retirements.

In 1993 Ferrari launched a one-model race series in Europe for 348 road car owners, who could buy a safety kit to upgrade their car for competition use. This proved extremely popular, and the scheme spread across the world in the following years, initially with the 348s and then the succeeding F355 models, climaxing in Italy for the end-of-season final. There was also a small series of 348 'Competizione' cars produced for national racing, and a pair of 348GTC-LM cars were prepared and raced in the 1994 Le Mans race by the Italian and Spanish Ferrari clubs. This is just one of the many colourful liveries worn by these cars, which added to the spectacle.

(Opposite top) By the start of the 1994 season Ferrari had gone for three years without a single victory in F1. The driver line-up was retained, to provide some continuity, and the car for the season was the 412T1, which was updated to 'B' specification after six races. There was a return to an all-red paint scheme, and there were changes to the body and nose profiles compared to the car's predecessor, though it was powered by a similar 3.5-litre V12 engine. Jean Alesi recorded a second place and three thirds, while Gerhard Berger posted the first victory after the long wait, plus three second places, and two thirds, which netted both him and Ferrari third place in the respective championships.

(Opposite bottom) The 3.5-litre V12 engine of a 412T1B with the air box removed, showing a very complex and sophisticated piece of machinery.

At the instigation of Piero Ferrari, a sports prototype project was undertaken, which was subcontracted to the Dallara concern for construction purposes. The result of this was the 333SP model which appeared in 1994. It was powered by a normally aspirated 4-litre V12 engine producing a claimed 650bhp, coupled to a five-speed sequential change gearbox. The model created great interest as it was intended only for private entrants, with no works participation. Since its inception it has proved to be a formidable piece of equipment, and the number of outright victories (see Appendix II) shows how good a car it has been, despite strong opposition from other marques. This is one of the early cars in the series, chassis number 005, of the French Pilot-sponsored team competing at Le Mans in 1998.

The F40LM made its comeback on the international stage in 1994 with the introduction of the BPR GT race series. It continued to race in this series for the next three years, proving very competitive, although often suffering minor maladies that kept it out of the top spot. This is the 'Pilot' car, chassis number 74045, which won at Anderstorp in 1995, seen here during the 1996 Le Mans race.

The 412T2 engine type number 044/1 was Ferrari's last V12 F1 engine of the 1990s, before the change to the more compact V10 configuration.

(Opposite top) For the 1995 season the regulations decreed a maximum engine capacity of 3 litres, and Ferrari produced the V12-engined 412T2 model for Alesi and Berger, while the other main protagonists had V10 power, courtesy of Renault. It was another single-victory year for Ferrari, when Jean Alesi took his long-awaited first grand prix victory in Canada, after having come close on a number of occasions. He also came second four times. The consistent points scored by both drivers during the season meant that Ferrari finished third in the Constructors' Championship.

(Opposite bottom) The privateer F40LMs of the team run by Luciano della Noce were upgraded to F40GT-E models in 1995, the 'E' standing for 'Evoluzione', and they raced in this form in the BPR series and at Le Mans, where brightly hued chassis number 90001 is seen in action.

It was all change at Ferrari in 1996, with a fresh driver line-up headed by the current World Champion Michael Schumacher, with Eddie Irvine as his team-mate. On the car front Ferrari had taken the V10 engine route, and produced the F310 model. In mid-season the team hit reliability problems, which fortunately were quickly resolved, and in Schumacher's hands the car proved very competitive when running properly. By the end of the season he had recorded four wins, five seconds and two third places, giving Ferrari their most successful season for a long time. The car was initially raced in low nose form, but the high nose seen here was soon adopted as standard wear.

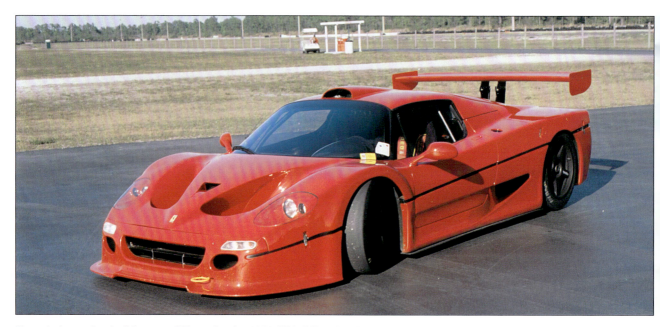

Ferrari planned to build a new GT car for the 1997 FIA GT series. It was to be based on the limited edition F50 road car, and would be called the F50GT1. However, after a prototype had been built and tested it was decided to abort the project, as it would divert important technological resources from the F1 effort. A total of three examples were built, this being the first, chassis number 001.

The F50GT1 from the rear. Beneath the rear deck is the 4.7-litre V12 engine that produced a claimed 750bhp at 10,500 rpm.

The F40GT-E and LM models entered their last season of top-level competition in 1996, and the della Noce team cars once again proved to be very quick, but minor problems frequently kept them off the podium. They did take victory at Anderstorp, as had the F40LM of the French Pilot team in 1995, recording their only win of the year. This is their chassis number 90001 at Spa-Francorchamps.

The F310 was developed into the F310B for the 1997 season, now with a seven-speed transverse gearbox, and a claimed 650+bhp. The main visual differences were in the shape of the radiator intakes in the side pods, the cockpit sides and the shape of the air box. The driver pairing remained the same, and Michael Schumacher took five wins, with the championship going down to the final race in Portugal, nominated the European Grand Prix. However, in a spur of the moment decision Schumacher tried an ill-judged blocking move on Villeneuve, and came out the loser not only on the track but also later, when he was stripped of his Championship points.

For the 1998 season the F1 contender became the F300 model, which is very difficult to distinguish visually from its predecessor, particularly as on both cars different trim tab configurations were used during the respective seasons. The most distinctive identifying feature is the lack of extended wing end plates into the side pods on the F300. The claimed power output was up to 700+bhp from the V10 engine. The drivers remained unchanged, so it was Irvine backing Schumacher for a third Ferrari attempt at the title. Despite six victories by Schumacher during the season, both Drivers' and Constructors' titles eluded them, runner-up spot in both being scant consolation for a long and hard-fought season.

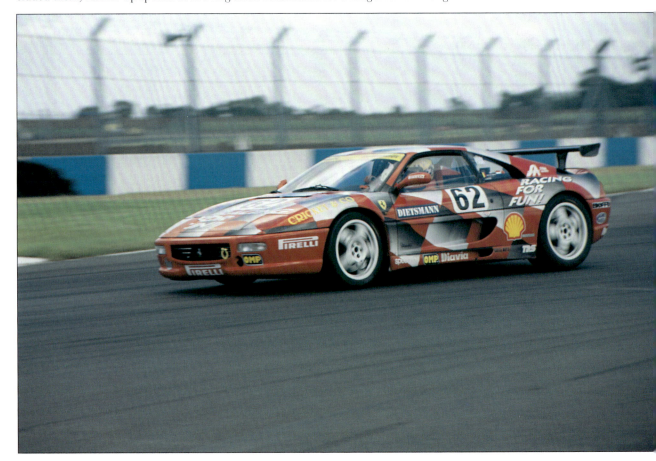

When the F355 model was announced, the Challenge series encompassed both the preceding 348 model and the F355 for the 1995 season. Thereafter it was solely for the F355 model, with the only major change being the removal of interior trim (on safety grounds), the addition of a perforated rear engine bay grille to aid heat dissipation, and the provision of a rear wing in 1998. They continued to provide a colourful high-speed spectacle with some close racing.

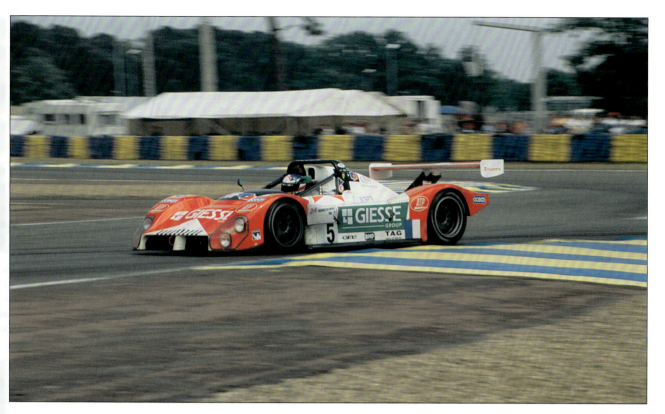

The 333SP sports racing models continued to have a successful career through to the end of the decade. They tasted victory in the hands of various private teams in Europe and the USA, in a variety of attractive liveries, two examples of which are shown here at Le Mans in 1998 – which was one of the few venues where they did not shine. Note also the detail body differences between these late series cars and the example shown earlier. Several teams tried their own aerodynamic tweaks, as with the long tail on car number 5 (chassis number 022), and the central fin on the air box of car number 3 (chassis number 019).

The final appearance of a 333SP in the Le Mans 24 Hour Race was this single entry from the JB-Giesse team, chassis number 030, in the 1999 event in which it retired.

The final Ferrari F1 car of the twentieth century was the F399 model. This V10-engined machine took Eddie Irvine to within a whisker of the Drivers' title after Michael Schumacher's mid-season crash on the first lap of the British Grand Prix at Silverstone had put paid to his title hopes. It did bring Ferrari the Constructors' Championship, with a total of six victories and numerous podium finishes. Mika Salo was drafted into the team to back Eddie Irvine until Michael Schumacher was fit to return in the penultimate grand prix of the season in Malaysia. This is Michael Schumacher at the Ferrari end-of-season Challenge meeting at Vallelunga.

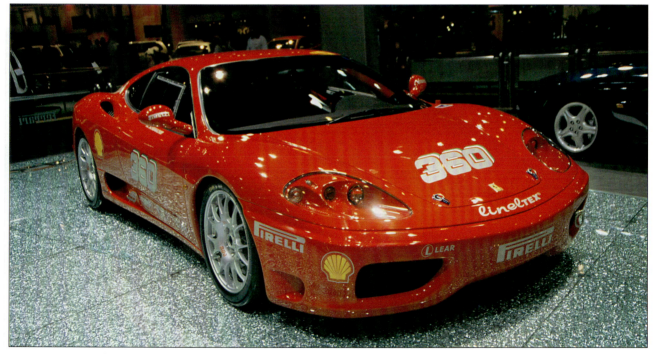

The 360 Modena was presented in 1999 as the replacement for the F355 series. In the middle of the year a Challenge version was announced for the 2000 single-model race series. Strictly speaking it would be two models during the year 2000, as the preceding F355 Challenge cars would be allowed to compete in a separate category. In early races of the season the new model has been up to three seconds a lap quicker on some circuits than its predecessor. The 3.6-litre V8 engine, producing 400bhp, is coupled to a six-speed gearbox utilising the 'F1' paddle change on the steering column.

The F1-2000 Formula One contender for the 2000 season and its compact 3-litre V10 engine. The driver line-up is Michael Schumacher and Rubens Barichello.

Model Types and Years of Production/Racing

Single-Seaters

1948	125 GP, 166F2
1949	125 F1, 166 F2, 166 FL
1950	125 F1, 375 F1, 166 F2, 166 FL
1951	375 F1, 212 F1, 625 F1, T/Wall SP #1*.
1952	500 F2, 625 F1, 375 Indy, T/Wall SP #2*.
1953	500 F2, 625 F1, 553 F2 Squalo, 375 Indy
1954	625 F1, 553 F1, 375 Indy
1955	625 F1, 555 F1
1956	D50 F1, 625/750, 555/860
1957	801 F1, 246 F1, 156 F2
1958	246/58 F1, 256 F1, 156 F2, 625 Tasman, 296 MI, 412 MI
1959	246/59 F1, 256 F1, 156 F2
1960	246/60 F1, 156 F2
1961	156 F1, 246 F1/250 Tasman
1962	156 F1
1963	156 F1, 156 Aero F1
1964	156 Aero F1, 158 F1, 1512 F1
1965	158 F1, 1512 F1
1966	312 F1, 246T F1
1967	312 F1, 166 F2
1968	312 F1, 246T/68, 166F2
1969	312 F1, 246T/69, 166 F2
1970	312B F1, 246T/69
1971	312B F1, 312B2 F1
1972	312B2 F1
1973	312B2 F1, 312B3 F1
1974	312B3 F1
1975	312T F1
1976	312T F1, 312T2 F1
1977	312T2 F1
1978	312T2 F1, 312T3 F1
1979	312T4 F1
1980	312T5 F1
1981	126CK F1
1982	126C2 F1
1983	126C2 F1, 126C3 F1
1984	126C4 F1
1985	156/85 F1
1986	F1-86 F1
1987	F1-87 F1
1988	F1-87/88C F1
1989	640 F1
1990	641 F1, 641/2 F1
1991	642 F1, 643 F1
1992	F92A F1, F92AT F1
1993	F93A F1
1994	412T1 F1, 412T1B F1
1995	412T2 F1
1996	F310 F1
1997	F310B F1
1998	F300 F1
1999	F399 F1
2000	F1-2000

Sports Racing and GT Cars

1947	125S, 159S, 166 Spider Corsa
1948	166S, 166 Spider Corsa, 166MM Barch'
1949	166 Spider Corsa, 166MM Barch' + Berl'
1950	166MM Barch' + Berl', 195S Berl', 275S
1951	212 Inter, 212 Export, 340 America
1952	212 Inter, 212 Export, 225S, 250S, 340 America, 340 Mexico
1953	166MM/53, 250MM, 340MM, 375MM, 625TF, 735S
1954	250 Europa GT, 250 Monza, 375MM, 375 Plus, 500 Mondial, 750 Monza
1955	118LM, 121LM, 500 Mondial, 750 Monza, 857S
1956	250GT LWB, 290MM, 410S, 860 Monza, 500TR, 625LM
1957	250GT LWB, 315S, 335S, 500TRC
1958	250GT LWB, 250TR, 412 Monza
1959	250GT LWB, 250TR/59
1960	250GT SWB, 250TR/60,196S, 246S
1961	250GT SWB, 246SP, 250TRI/61
1962	250GTO, 196SP, 286SP, 248SP, 268SP, 330TRI/LM
1963	250GTO, 330LM, 250P, 330P
1964	250GTO, 250LM, 275GTB/C, 275P, 330P
1965	250LM, 275GTB/C, 166P, 206P, 275P2, 330P2, 365P
1966	275GTB/C, 206S, 330P3, 365P
1967	206S, 412P, 330P4, 350 Canam
1968	612 Canam
1969	212E, 312P, 712 Canam
1970	512S
1971	365GTB/4C**, 312PB, 512M
1972	365GTB/4C**, 312PB
1973	365GTB/4C**, 312PB
1975	365GT4/BB**
1976	365GT4/BB**
1977	365GT4/BB**
1978	512BB/LM**
1979	512BB/LM**
1980	512BB/LM**, 308 GTB/M***, 308GTB Gp4***
1981	512BB/LM**, 308GTB Gp4***
1982	512BB/LM**
1988	F40LM***
1989	F40LM***
1990	F40LM***
1993	348GT/C***
1994	333SP****, F40LM***, 348GT/C-LM***
1995	333SP****, F40LM***
1996	333SP****, F40GT-E***, F50 GT1
1997	333SP***
1998	333SP***
1999	333SP***

**Built/Prepared by Ferrari 'Assistenza Clienti', Modena.
***Built/Prepared by Michelotto of Padova.
****Built/Prepared by Dallara.

* Ferrari modified by Vandervell Products Ltd

Appendix II

Annual Review of Major Race Results, 1947–99

YEAR/VENUE	DRIVER(S)	MODEL	RESULT
1947			
Rome GP	Franco Cortese	125S	1st
1948			
Mille Miglia	Biondetti/Navone	166S	1st
Targa Florio	Biondetti/Troubetzkoy	166S	1st
Bari GP F2	Chico Landi	166	1st
Paris 12 Hrs	Chinetti/Selsdon	166I	1st
Florence GP F2	Raymond Sommer	166	1st
	Clemente Biondetti	166	2nd
1949			
Mille Miglia	Biondetti/Salani	166MM	1st
	Bonetto/Carpani	166MM	2nd
Targa Florio	Biondetti/Benedetti	166MM	1st
Le Mans 24 Hrs	Chinetti/Selsdon	166MM	1st
Spa 24 Hrs	Chinetti/Lucas	166MM	1st
Swiss GP	Alberto Ascari	125	1st
	Luigi Villoresi	125	2nd
Zandvoort GP	Luigi Villoresi	125	1st
International Trophy, Silverstone	Alberto Ascari	125	1st
Italian GP (Euro)	Alberto Ascari	125	1st
Czech GP, Brno	Peter Whitehead	125	1st
Autodromo GP, F2 (NC), Monza	Juan Manuel Fangio	166	1st
Brussels GP F2	Luigi Villoresi	166	1st
Luxembourg GP F2	Luigi Villoresi	166	1st
Rome GP F2	Luigi Villoresi	166	1st
	Piero Taruffi	166	2nd
	Franco Cortese	166	3rd
	Felice Bonetto	166	4th
Bari GP F2	Alberto Ascari	166	1st
	Franco Cortese	166	2nd
	Felice Bonetto	166	3rd
	Luigi Villoresi	166	4th
	Roberto Vallone	166	5th
Naples GP F2	Roberto Vallone	166	1st
	Felice Bonetto	166	2nd
1950			
Mille Miglia	Marzotto/Crosara	195S	1st
	Serafini/Salani	195S	2nd
Jersey	Peter Whitehead	125	1st
Ulster Trophy	Peter Whitehead	125	1st
Barcelona	Alberto Ascari	375 FI	1st
	Dorino Serafini	375 FI	2nd
	Piero Taruffi	340 FI	3rd
Modena GP F2	Alberto Ascari	166	1st
Mons F2	Alberto Ascari	166	1st
Autodromo GP F2 Monza	Luigi Villoresi	166	1st
Swiss GP F2	Raymond Sommer	166	1st
Rome GP F2	Alberto Ascari	166	1st
	Luigi Villoresi	166	2nd
	Roberto Vallone	166	3rd
Reims F2	Alberto Ascari	166	1st
Erlen F2	Luigi Villoresi	166	1st
Nurburgring F2	Alberto Ascari	166	1st
Garda F2	Alberto Ascari	166	1st
	Dorino Serafini	166	2nd
1951			
British GP	Froilan Gonzalez	375 FI	1st
German GP	Alberto Ascari	375 FI	1st
Italian GP	Alberto Ascari	375 FI	1st
	Froilan Gonzalez	375 FI	2nd
Mille Miglia	Villoresi/Cassani	340A	1st
Carrera Panamericana	Taruffi/Chinetti	212E	1st
	Ascari/Villoresi	212E	2nd
Syracuse GP (NC)	Luigi Villoresi	375 FI	1st
	Dorino Serafini	212 FI	2nd
	Rudolf Fischer	212 FI	3rd
Pau GP (NC)	Luigi Villoresi	375 FI	1st
Rouen GP (NC)	Giannino Marzotto	166 F2	1st
San Remo (NC)	Alberto Ascari	375 FI	1st
	Dorino Serafini	375 FI	2nd
	Rudolf Fischer	212 FI	3rd
International Trophy, Silverstone (NC)	Reg Parnell	375TW	1st
Pescara GP (NC)	Froilan Gonzalez	375 FI	1st
Marseilles F2 (NC)	Luigi Villoresi	166 F2	1st
Autodromo GP F2 (NC) Monza	Alberto Ascari	166 F2	1st
Rome GP F2 (NC)	Mario Raffaeli	166 F2	1st
Rouen GP F2 (NC)	Giannino Marzotto	166 F2	1st
Naples F2 (NC)	Alberto Ascari	500 F2	1st
Modena GP F2 (NC)	Froilan Gonzalez	166 F2	2nd

1952

Event	Driver	Car	Position
Swiss GP	Piero Taruffi	500 F2	1st
	Rudolph Fischer	500 F2	2nd
Belgian GP	Alberto Ascari	500 F2	1st
	Giuseppe Farina	500 F2	2nd
French GP	Alberto Ascari	500 F2	1st
	Giuseppe Farina	500 F2	2nd
	Piero Taruffi	500 F2	3rd
British GP	Alberto Ascari	500 F2	1st
	Piero Taruffi	500 F2	2nd
German GP	Alberto Ascari	500 F2	1st
	Giuseppe Farina	500 F2	2nd
	Rudolph Fischer	500 F2	3rd
	Piero Taruffi	500 F2	4th
Dutch GP	Alberto Ascari	500 F2	1st
	Giuseppe Farina	500 F2	2nd
	Luigi Villoresi	500 F2	3rd
Italian GP	Alberto Ascari	500 F2	1st
Mille Miglia (Sport)	Bracco/Rolfo	250S	1st
Syracuse GP (NC)	Alberto Ascari	500 F2	1st
	Piero Taruffi	500 F2	2nd
	Giuseppe Farina	500 F2	3rd
Pau GP (NC)	Alberto Ascari	500 F2	1st
Marseilles GP (NC)	Alberto Ascari	500 F2	1st
Naples GP (NC)	Alberto Ascari	500 F2	1st
Paris GP (NC)	Piero Taruffi	500 F2	1st
Autodromo GP F2 (NC), Monza	Giuseppe Farina	500 F2	2nd
	Andre Simon	500 F2	3rd
Sables D'Olonne (NC)	Luigi Villoresi	375 F1	1st
Comminges (NC)	Simon/Ascari	375TW	1st
	Giuseppe Farina	500 F2	2nd
Modena GP (NC)	Luigi Villoresi	500 F2	1st
Avus GP (NC)	Rudolf Fischer	500 F2	1st
Eifelrennen, Nurburgring (NC)	Rudolf Fischer	500 F2	2nd
Turin F. Libre	Luigi Villoresi	375 F1	1st
	Piero Taruffi	625 F1	2nd
Goodwood F. Libre	Froilan Gonzalez	375TW	1st
Albi F. Libre	Louis Rosier	375 F1	1st
	Chico Landi	375 F1	2nd
Ulster Trophy F. Libre	Piero Taruffi	375 F1	1st
Silverstone F. Libre	Piero Taruffi	375TW	1st
	Luigi Villoresi	375 F1	2nd
	Chico Landi	375 F1	3rd
Monaco GP (Sports)	Vittorio Marzotto	225S	1st
	Eugenio Castellotti	225S	2nd
	Stagnoli/Biondetti	225S	3rd
	Lucas/Simon	225S	4th
	'Pagnibon'	225S	5th
Coppa Inter Europa, Monza (Sports)	Bruno Sterzi	212E	1st
	Franco Cornacchia	212E	2nd
	Bianca Maria Piazza	195I	3rd
Pescara 12 Hrs (Sports)	Marzotto P./Bracco	250S	1st
	Cornacchia/Biondetti	225S	2nd
	Piotti/Mallucci	225S	3rd
Bari GP (Sports)	Chico Landi	195S	1st
	Tom Cole	225S	2nd
	Eugenio Castellotti	225S	3rd

1953

Event	Driver	Car	Position
Argentine GP	Alberto Ascari	500 F2	1st
	Luigi Villoresi	500 F2	2nd
Dutch GP	Alberto Ascari	500 F2	1st
	Giuseppe Farina	500 F2	2nd
Belgian GP	Alberto Ascari	500 F2	1st
	Luigi Villoresi	500 F2	2nd
French GP	Mike Hawthorn	500 F2	1st
British GP	Alberto Ascari	500 F2	1st
German GP	Giuseppe Farina	500 F2	1st
Swiss GP	Alberto Ascari	500 F2	1st
	Giuseppe Farina	500 F2	2nd
	Mike Hawthorn	500 F2	3rd
Mille Miglia	Marzotto G./Crosara	340MM	1st
Spa 24 Hrs	Farina/Hawthorn	340MM	1st
Nurburgring 1000km	Ascari/Farina	375MM	1st
Buenos Aires City GP	Giuseppe Farina	625 F1	1st
	Luigi Villoresi	625 F1	2nd
	Mike Hawthorn	625 F1	3rd
Albi GP F. Libre	Louis Rosier	375 F1	1st
Goodwood F. Libre	Piero Taruffi	375TW	1st
Silverstone F. Libre	Giuseppe Farina	375TW	1st
Goodwood F. Libre	Mike Hawthorn	375TW	1st
Pau GP (NC)	Alberto Ascari	500 F2	1st
	Mike Hawthorn	500 F2	2nd
Bordeaux (NC)	Alberto Ascari	500 F2	1st
	Luigi Villoresi	500 F2	2nd
Rouen GP (NC)	Giuseppe Farina	500 F2	1st
	Mike Hawthorn	625 F1	2nd
International Trophy, Silverstone (NC)	Mike Hawthorn	500 F2	1st
Avus GP (NC)	Alberto Ascari	500 F2	1st
Ulster Trophy (NC)	Mike Hawthorn	500 F2	2nd
Naples (NC)	Alberto Ascari	500 F2	1st
Autodromo GP (Sports) (NC) Monza	Luigi Villoresi	250MM	2nd

1954

Event	Driver	Car	Position
Pescara 12 Hrs	Hawthorn/Maglioli	375MM	1st
British GP	Froilan Gonzalez	625 F1	1st
	Mike Hawthorn	625 F1	2nd
Spanish GP	Mike Hawthorn	553 F1	1st

Event	Driver(s)	Car	Position
Buenos Aires 1000km	Farina/Maglioli	375MM	1st
	Schell/de Portago	250MM	2nd
Le Mans 24 Hrs	Trintignant/Gonzalez	375 Plus	1st
Carrera Panamericana	Maglioli	375 Plus	1st
	Hill P./Ginther	375MM	2nd
Buenos Aires City GP	Maurice Trintignant	625 FI	1st
Syracuse GP (NC)	Giuseppe Farina	625 FI	1st
	Maurice Trintignant	625 FI	2nd
Bordeaux GP (NC)	Froilan Gonzalez	625 FI	1st
Bari GP (NC)	Froilan Gonzalez	625 FI	1st
	Maurice Trintignant	625 FI	2nd
Caen GP (NC)	Maurice Trintignant	625 FI	1st
Rouen GP (NC)	Maurice Trintignant	625 FI	1st
International Trophy, Silverstone	Froilan Gonzalez	553 FI	1st
1955			
Imola GP (NC)	Umberto Maglioli	500 Mondial	1st
Goodwood F. Libre 1	Peter Collins	375TW	1st
Goodwood F. Libre 2	Peter Collins	375TW	1st
Snetterton F. Libre	Peter Collins	375TW	1st
Monaco GP	Maurice Trintignant	625 FI	1st
Buenos Aires 1000km	Saenz-Valiente/Ibenez	375 Plus	1st
	Najurieta/Rivero	375MM	2nd
Targa Mugello (Sports)	Umberto Maglioli	750 Monza	1st
1956			
Argentine GP	Musso/Fangio	L-F D50	1st
Belgian GP	Peter Collins	L-F D50	1st
	Paul Frere	L-F D50	2nd
French GP	Peter Collins	L-F D50	1st
	Eugenio Castellotti	L-F D50	2nd
British GP	Juan Manuel Fangio	L-F D50	1st
	de Portago/Collins	L-F D50	2nd
German GP	Juan Manuel Fangio	L-F D50	1st
Mendoza GP (NC)	Juan Manuel Fangio	L-F D50	1st
Syracuse GP (NC)	Juan Manuel Fangio	L-F D50	1st
	Luigi Musso	L-F D50	2nd
	Peter Collins	L-F D50	3rd
Sebring 12 Hrs	Fangio/Castellotti	860 Monza	1st
	Musso/Schell	860 Monza	2nd
Mille Miglia	Castellotti	290MM	1st
	Collins/Klementaski	860 Monza	2nd
	Musso	860 Monza	3rd
	Fangio	290MM	4th
	Gendebien/Washer	250GT	5th
Swedish GP (Sports)	Hill P./Trintignant	290MM	1st
	Collins/von Trips	290MM	2nd
	Hawthorn/Hamilton/de Portago	290MM	3rd
	Kvarnstrom/Lundgren	250GT	4th
	Borgefors/Hammarlund	250GT	5th
Rouen GP (NC) (Sports)	Eugenio Castellotti	--	1st
Tour de France	de Portago/Nelson	250GT	1st
1957			
Buenos Aires 1000km	Gregory/Perdisa/Castellotti/Musso	290MM	1st
Mille Miglia	Taruffi	315S	1st
	von Trips	315S	2nd
	Gendebien/Washer	250GT	3rd
Venezuela GP (Sports)	Collins/Hill P.	335S	1st
	Hawthorn/Musso	335S	2nd
	von Trips/Seidel	250TR	3rd
	Gendebien/Trintignant	250TR	4th
Australian GP (NC)	Davison/Patterson	625	1st
Syracuse GP (NC)	Peter Collins	801	1st
	Luigi Musso	801	2nd
Naples GP (NC)	Peter Collins	801	1st
	Mike Hawthorn	D50A/SS	2nd
	Luigi Musso	156 F2	3rd
Reims GP (NC)	Luigi Musso	L-F D50	1st
Reims 12 Hrs (GT)	Frere/Gendebien	250GT	1st
	Hill P./Seidel	250GT	2nd
	Munaron/Madero	250GT	3rd
	Papais/Crivellari	250GT	4th
	Luglio/Picard	250GT	5th
Tour de France	Gendebien/Bianchi	250GT	1st
	Trintignant/Picard	250GT	2nd
	Lucas/Malle	250GT	3rd
Coppa Inter Europa, Monza (GT)	Camillo Luglio	250GT	1st
	Edoardo Lualdi-Gabardi	250GT	2nd
	Luigi Taramazzo	250GT	3rd
1958			
French GP	Mike Hawthorn	Dino 246	1st
British GP	Peter Collins	Dino 246	1st
	Mike Hawthorn	Dino 246	2nd
Buenos Aires 1000km	Hill P./Collins	250TR	1st
	von Trips/Gendebien/Hawthorn/Musso	250TR	2nd
Sebring 12 Hrs	Hill P./Collins	250TR	1st
	Gendebien/Musso	250TR	2nd
Targa Florio	Gendebien/Musso	250TR	1st
Le Mans 24 Hrs	Gendebien/Hill P.	250TR	1st
Australian GP (NC)	Lex Davison	625	1st
Syracuse GP (NC)	Luigi Musso	Dino 246	1st
Daily Express Trophy, Silverstone (NC)	Peter Collins	Dino 246	1st
Eifelrennen/ Nurburgring (GT)	Wolfgang Seidel	250GT	1st
Glover Trophy, Goodwood (NC)	Mike Hawthorn	Dino 246	1st
Reims 12 Hrs (GT)	Frere/Gendebien	250GT	1st
	Mairesse/'Haldeaux' ('Beurlys')	250GT	2nd
	Noblet/Peron	250GT	3rd
Tour de France	Gendebien/Bianchi	250GT	1st
	Trintignant/Picard	250GT	2nd
	Silva Ramos/Estager	250GT	3rd

Event	Driver(s)	Car	Position
Coppa Inter Europa, Monza (GT)	Schell/Peron	250GT	4th
	Schild/La Geneste	250GT	5th
	Luigi Taramazzo	250GT	1st
	Carlo Leto de Priolo	250GT	2nd
	Edoardo Lualdi-Gabardi	250GT	3rd
Pau 3 Hrs (GT)	Olivier Gendebien	250GT	1st
	Wolfgang Seidel	250GT	2nd
	Gino Munaron	250GT	3rd
Spa (GT)	Nano da Silva Ramos	250GT	1st
	Wolfgang Seidel	250 GT	2nd
1959			
French GP	Tony Brooks	Dino 246	1st
	Phil Hill	Dino 246	2nd
German GP	Tony Brooks	Dino 246	1st
	Dan Gurney	Dino 246	2nd
	Phil Hill	Dino 246	3rd
Sebring 12 Hrs	Gurney/Daigh/Hill P./Gendebien	250TR	1st
	Behra/Allison	250TR	2nd
Monza Lottery (GT)	Alfonso Thiele	250GT	1st
	Carlo Mario Abate	250GT	2nd
	Willy Mairesse	250GT	3rd
Tour de France	Gendebien/Bianchi	250GT	1st
	Mairesse/Berger	250GT	2nd
	Schild/de la Geneste	250GT	3rd
Coppa Inter Europa, Monza (GT)	Alfonso Thiele	250GT	1st
	Carlo Mario Abate	250GT	2nd
	Pierre Noblet	250GT	3rd
	Ottavio Randaccio	250GT	4th
1960			
Italian GP	Phil Hill	Dino 246	1st
	Richie Ginther	Dino 246	2nd
	Willie Mairesse	Dino 246	3rd
Buenos Aires 1000km	Hill P./Allison	250TR	1st
	von Trips/Ginther	250TR	2nd
Le Mans 24 Hrs	Frere/Gendebien	250TR	1st
	Rodriguez R./Pilette	250TR	2nd
Monthlery 1000km	Gendebien/Bianchi	250GT	1st
	Mairesse/von Trips	250GT	2nd
	Schlesser/Simon	250GT	3rd
	Dumay/Tavano	250GT	4th
Tourist Trophy(GT)	Whitehead/Taylor	250GT	5th
	Stirling Moss	250GT	1st
Tour de France	Mairesse/Berger	250GT	1st
	Dumay/Schlesser	250GT	2nd
	Tavano/Martin	250GT	3rd
Coppa Inter Europa, Monza (GT)	Carlo Mario Abate	250GT	1st
	Jean Guichet	250GT	2nd
	Miro Toselli	250GT	3rd
Spa (GT)	Willy Mairesse	250 GT	1st
1961			
Dutch GP	Wolfgang von Trips	156	1st
	Phil Hill	156	2nd
Belgian GP	Phil Hill	156	1st
	Wolfgang von Trips	156	2nd
	Richie Ginther	156	3rd
	Olivier Gendebien	156	4th
French GP	Giancarlo Baghetti	156	1st
British GP	Wolfgang von Trips	156	1st
	Phil Hill	156	2nd
	Richie Ginther	156	3rd
Italian GP	Phil Hill	156	1st
Syracuse GP (NC)	Giancarlo Baghetti	156	1st
Naples GP (NC)	Giancarlo Baghetti	156	1st
Sebring 12 Hrs	Hill P./Gendebien	250TR	1st
	von Trips/Mairesse/Baghetti/Ginther	250TR	2nd
	Rodriguez, P. & R.	250TR	3rd
	Sharp/Hissom	250TR	4th
Targa Florio	von Trips/Gendebien	Dino 246SP	1st
Le Mans 24 Hrs	Gendebien/Hill P.	250TR	1st
	Mairesse/Parkes	250TR	2nd
	Noblet/Guichet	250TR	3rd*
Pescara 4 Hrs	Bandini/Scarlatti	250TR	1st
Monthery 1000km	Rodriguez, P. & R.	250GT	1st
	Mairesse/Bianchi	250GT	2nd
	Trintignant/Vaccarella 250GT	3rd	3rd
	Dumay/Schlesser	250GT	4th
	Abate/Davis	250GT	5th
Solitude GP (F2)	Wolfgang von Trips	Dino 156	1st
Tourist Trophy (GT)	Stirling Moss	250GT	1st
Tour de France	Mairesse/Berger	250GT	1st
	Gendebien/Bianchi	250GT	2nd
	Trintignant/Cavrois	250GT	3rd
	Berney/Gretener	250GT	4th
Coppa Inter Europa, Monza (GT)	Pierre Noblet	250GT	1st
Spa GP (GT)	Willy Mairesse	250GT	1st
1962			
Sebring 12 Hrs	Bonnier/Bianchi	250TR	1st
	Hill P./Gendebien	250GTO	2nd*
Targa Florio	Mairesse/Gendebien/Rodriguez R.	Dino 246SP	1st
Nurburgring 1000km	Bandini/Baghetti	Dino 196SP	2nd
	Hill P./Gendebien	Dino 246SP	1st
Le Mans 24 Hrs	Mairesse/Parkes	330GTO	2nd
	Gendebien/Hill P.	330TRI	1st
Coppa Inter Europa, Monza (GT)	Noblet/Guichet	250GTO	2nd*
	'Elde'/'Beurlys'	250GTO	3rd
Monthery 1000km	Rodriguezi P. & R.	250GTO	1st
	Surtees/Parkes	250GTO	2nd

Event	Driver(s)	Car	Position
Brussels GP (NC)	Davis/Scarfiotti	250GT	3rd
	Guichet/Noblet	250GTO	4th
	Mairesse/Bianchi	250GTO	5th
Mediterranean GP	Simon/Berger	250GT	6th
Enna-Pergusa, FI (NC)	Willy Mairesse	156	1st
Avus GP (NC) (GT)	Lorenzo Bandini	156	1st
	Giancarlo Baghetti	156	2nd
	Edgar Berney	250GT	1st
Tourist Trophy (GT)	Innes Ireland	250GTO	1st
	Graham Hill	250GTO	2nd
	Mike Parkes	250GTO	3rd
Tour de France	Simon/Dupeyron	250GTO	1st
	Oreiller/Schlesser	250GTO	2nd
	Darville/Langlois van Ophem	250GTO	3rd
	Piper/Margulies	250GTO	4th
	de la Geneste/Burglin	250GT	5th
Spa GP (GT)	Edgar Berney	250GT	1st
	Pierre Noblet	250GT	2nd
	Jo Berger	250GT	3rd
	Robert Crevits	250GT	4th
1963			
German GP	John Surtees	156	1st
Enna-Pergusa, FI (NC)	John Surtees	156	1st
Rand GP (NC)	John Surtees	156	1st
	Lorenzo Bandini	156	2nd
Sebring 12 Hrs	Surtees/Scarfiotti	250P	1st
	Mairesse/Vaccarella/Bandini	250P	2nd
	Rodriguez/Hill G.	330TRI	3rd
	Penske/Pabst	250GTO	4th*
	Abate/Bordeu	250GTO	5th
	Ireland/Ginther	250GTO	6th
Nurburgring 1000km	Surtees/Mairesse	250P	1st
	Guichet/Noblet	250GTO	2nd*
	Abate/Maglioli	250TR	3rd
Le Mans 24 Hrs	Bandini/Scarfiotti	250P	1st
	'Beurlys'/Langlois van Ophem	250GTO	2nd*
	Parkes/Maglioli	250P	3rd
	'Elde'/Dumay	330LM	4th
	Sears/Salmon	250GTO	5th
	Gregory/Piper	250GTO	6th
Canadian GP (Sports)	Pedro Rodriguez	250P	1st
Tourist Trophy (GT)	Graham Hill	250GTO	1st
Tour de France	Guichet/Behra	250GTO	1st
	Abate/Bianchi	250GTO	2nd
	Spinedi/Spinedi	250GTO	3rd
Spa 500km (GT)	Willy Mairesse	250GTO	1st
	Pierre Noblet	250GTO	2nd
	Jo Siffert	250GT	3rd
	Langlois van Ophem	250GT	4th
	Chris Kerrison	250GT	5th
	Plaut	250GT	6th
1964			
German GP	John Surtees	158	1st
Austrian GP	Lorenzo Bandini	158	1st
Italian GP	John Surtees	158	1st
Syracuse GP(NC)	John Surtees	158	1st
	Lorenzo Bandini	156	2nd
Daytona Continental	Hill P./Rodriguez P.	250GTO	1st
	Piper/Bianchi	250GTO	2nd
	Grossman/Hansgen	250GTO	3rd
Sebring 12 Hrs	Parkes/Maglioli	275P	1st
	Scarfiotti/Vaccarella	275P	2nd
	Surtees/Bandini	330P	3rd
Spa 500km (GT)	Mike Parkes	250GTO	1st
	Jean Guichet	250GTO	2nd
	Lorenzo Bandini	250GTO	3rd
	David Piper	250GTO	4th
	Chris Kerrison	250GT	5th
	Langlois van Ophem	250GTO	6th
Nurburgring 1000km	Scarfiotti/Vaccarella	275P	1st
	Parkes/Guichet	250GTO	2nd
Le Mans 24 Hrs	Guichet/Vaccarella	275P	1st
	Bonnier/Hill G.	330P	2nd
	Surtees/Bandini	330P	3rd
Reims 12 Hrs	Bonnier/Hill G.	250LM	1st
	Surtees/Bandini	250LM	2nd
	Parkes/Scarfiotti	250GTO	3rd
	Piper/Maggs	250GTO	4th
Tourist Trophy	Graham Hill	330P	1st
Paris 1000km	David Piper	250LM	2nd
	Bonnier/Hill G.	330P	2nd
	Rodriguez P./Schlesser	250GTO	2nd
Canadian GP (Sports)	Pedro Rodriguez	330P	--
Tour de France	Bianchi/Berger	250GTO	1st
	Guichet/de Bourbon Parme	250GTO	2nd
1965			
Monza 1000km	Parkes/Guichet	275P2	1st
	Surtees/Scarfiotti	330P2	2nd
	Vaccarella/Bandini	275P2	2nd
Targa Florio	Willy Mairesse	250LM	1st
GP de Spa	David Piper	250LM	2nd
Nurburgring 1000km	Surtees/Scarfiotti	330P2	1st
	Parkes/Guichet	275P2	2nd
Le Mans 24 Hrs	Rindt/Gregory	250LM	1st
	Dumay/Gosselin	250LM	2nd
	Mairesse/'Beurlys'	275GTB/C	3rd
Reims 12 Hrs	Rodriguez P./Guichet	365P2	1st
	Surtees/Parkes	365P2	2nd
	Mairesse/'Beurlys'	250LM	3rd
Austrian GP (Sports)	Piper/Attwood	250LM	3rd
	Jochen Rindt	250LM	1st
Mugello (GT)	Nicodemi/Casoni	250LM	1st

1966

Race	Driver	Car	Pos.
Belgian GP	John Surtees	312	1st
Italian GP	Ludovico Scarfiotti	312	1st
Syracuse GP (NC)	Mike Parkes	312	2nd
	John Surtees	312	1st
Monza 1000km	Lorenzo Bandini	246T	2nd
	Surtees/Parkes	330P3	1st
Spa 1000km	Parkes/Scarfiotti	330P3	1st

1967

Race	Driver	Car	Pos.
Daytona 24 Hrs	Bandini/Amon	330P4	1st
	Parkes/Scarfiotti	330P4	2nd
	Rodriguez P./Guichet	412P	3rd
Monza 1000km	Bandini/Amon	330P4	1st
	Parkes/Scarfiotti	330P4	2nd
Syracuse GP (NC)	Mike Parkes	312	=1st
	Ludovico Scarfiotti	312	=1st
International Trophy, Silverstone	Mike Parkes	312	1st

1968

Race	Driver	Car	Pos.
French GP	Jacky Ickx	312	1st
Tasman Cup NZ GP	Chris Amon	246T	1st
Tasman Cup Levin	Chris Amon	246T	1st
Euro F2 Hockenheim	Tino Brambilla	Dino 166	1st
Euro F2 Rome GP	Tino Brambilla	Dino 166	1st
	Andrea de Adamich	Dino 166	2nd
Norisring 200 Miles	David Piper	330P4	1st
Solitude GP (Sports)	David Piper	330P4	1st

1969

Race	Driver	Car	Pos.
Tasman Cup NZ GP	Chris Amon	246T	1st
Tasman Cup Levin	Chris Amon	246T	1st
Tasman Cup AUS GP	Chris Amon	246T	1st
Tasman Cup Sandown Pk	Chris Amon	246T	1st

1970

Race	Driver	Car	Pos.
Austrian GP	Jacky Ickx	312B	1st
	Clay Regazzoni	312B	2nd
Italian GP	Clay Regazzoni	312B	1st
Canadian GP	Jacky Ickx	312B	1st
	Clay Regazzoni	312B	2nd
Mexican GP	Jacky Ickx	312B	1st
	Clay Regazzoni	312B	2nd
Sebring 12 Hrs	Giunti/Vaccarella/Andretti	512S	1st
Tasman Cup Levin	Graeme Lawrence	246T	1st
Fuji 200 Miles	Manfredini/Moretti	512S	1st
Kyalami 9 Hrs	Ickx/Giunti	512M	1st

1971

Race	Driver	Car	Pos.
South African GP	Mario Andretti	312B	1st
Dutch GP	Jacky Ickx	312B2	1st
Jochen Rindt Trophy Hockenheim (FI) (NC)	Jacky Ickx	312B	1st
Race of Champions (FI) (NC) Brands Hatch	Clay Regazzoni	312B2	1st

1972

Race	Driver	Car	Pos.
German GP	Jacky Ickx	312B2	1st
	Clay Regazzoni	312B2	2nd
Buenos Aires 1000km	Peterson/Schenken	312PB	2nd
	Regazzoni/Redman	312PB	1st
Daytona 6 Hrs	Ickx/Andretti	312PB	1st
	Peterson/Schenken	312PB	2nd
Sebring 12 Hrs	Ickx/Andretti	312PB	1st
	Peterson/Schenken	312PB	2nd
BOAC 1000km	Ickx/Andretti	312PB	1st
	Peterson/Schenken	312PB	2nd
Monza 1000km	Ickx/Regazzoni	312PB	1st
	Redman/Merzario	312PB	2nd
Spa 1000km	Ickx/Regazzoni	312PB	1st
Targa Florio	Merzario/Munari	312PB	1st
Nurburgring 1000km	Peterson/Schenken	312PB	1st
	Redman/Merzario	312PB	2nd
Osterreichring 1000km	Ickx/Redman	312PB	1st
	Marko/Pace	312PB	2nd
Watkins Glen 6 Hrs	Peterson/Schenken	312PB	3rd
	Merzario/Munari	312PB	4th

1973

Race	Driver	Car	Pos.
Monza 1000km	Ickx/Redman	312PB	1st
	Schenken/Reutemann	312PB	2nd
Nurburgring 1000km	Ickx/Redman	312PB	1st
	Merzario/Pace	312PB	2nd

1974

Race	Driver	Car	Pos.
Spanish GP	Niki Lauda	312B3	1st
Dutch GP	Clay Regazzoni	312B3	2nd
	Niki Lauda	312B3	1st
German GP	Clay Regazzoni	312B3	1st
	Niki Lauda	312B3	2nd

1975

Race	Driver	Car	Pos.
Monaco GP	Niki Lauda	312T	1st
Belgian GP	Niki Lauda	312T	1st
Swedish GP	Niki Lauda	312T	1st
French GP	Niki Lauda	312T	1st
Italian GP	Clay Regazzoni	312T	1st
United States GP	Niki Lauda	312T	1st
Swiss GP Dijon (NC)	Clay Regazzoni	312T	1st
International Trophy, Silverstone (NC)	Niki Lauda	312T	1st

1976

Race	Driver	Car	Pos.
South African GP	Niki Lauda	312T	1st
US GP West	Niki Lauda	312T	1st
Belgian GP	Clay Regazzoni	312T2	2nd
	Niki Lauda	312T2	1st
Monaco GP	Niki Lauda	312T2	2nd
British GP	Niki Lauda	312T2	1st

Year / Race	Driver	Car	Position
1977			
Brazilian GP	Carlos Reutemann	312T2	1st
South African GP	Niki Lauda	312T2	1st
German GP	Niki Lauda	312T2	1st
Dutch GP	Niki Lauda	312T2	1st
1978			
Brazilian GP	Carlos Reutemann	312T2	1st
US GP West	Carlos Reutemann	312T3	1st
British GP	Carlos Reutemann	312T3	1st
United States GP	Carlos Reutemann	312T3	1st
Canadian GP	Gilles Villeneuve	312T3	1st
1979			
South African GP	Jody Scheckter	312T4	1st
	Gilles Villeneuve	312T4	2nd
US GP West	Jody Scheckter	312T4	1st
	Gilles Villeneuve	312T4	2nd
Belgian GP	Jody Scheckter	312T4	1st
Monaco GP	Jody Scheckter	312T4	1st
Italian GP	Jody Scheckter	312T4	1st
	Gilles Villeneuve	312T4	2nd
Race of Champions (F1) (NC) Brands Hatch	Gilles Villeneuve	312T3	1st
1981			
Monaco GP	Gilles Villeneuve	126CK	1st
Spanish GP	Gilles Villeneuve	126CK	1st
1982			
San Marino GP	Didier Pironi	126C2	1st
	Gilles Villeneuve	126C2	2nd
Dutch GP	Didier Pironi	126C2	1st
German GP	Patrick Tambay	126C2	1st
1983			
San Marino GP	Patrick Tambay	126C2B	1st
Canadian GP	Rene Arnoux	126C2B	1st
German GP	Rene Arnoux	126C3	1st
Dutch GP	Rene Arnoux	126C3	1st
	Patrick Tambay	126C3	2nd
1984			
Belgian GP	Michele Alboreto	126C4	1st
1985			
Canadian GP	Michele Alboreto	156/85	1st
	Stefan Johansson	156/85	2nd
German GP	Michele Alboreto	156/85	1st
1987			
Japanese GP	Gerhard Berger	F1/87	1st
Australian GP	Gerhard Berger	F1/87	1st
	Michele Alboreto	F1/87	2nd
1988			
Italian GP	Gerhard Berger	F1/87/88C	1st
	Michele Alboreto	F1/87/88C	2nd

Year / Race	Driver	Car	Position
1989			
Brazilian GP	Nigel Mansell	640	1st
Hungarian GP	Nigel Mansell	640	1st
Portugese GP	Gerhard Berger	640	1st
1990			
Brazilian GP	Alain Prost	641	1st
Mexican GP	Alain Prost	641/2	1st
	Nigel Mansell	641/2	2nd
French GP	Alain Prost	641/2	1st
British GP	Alain Prost	641/2	1st
Portuguese GP	Nigel Mansell	641/2	1st
Spanish GP	Alain Prost	641/2	1st
	Nigel Mansell	641/2	2nd
1994			
German GP	Gerhard Berger	412T1B	1st
IMSA/WSC Road Atlanta	Jay Cochran	333SP	1st
	Moretti/Salazar	333SP	2nd
IMSA/WSC Lime Rock	Moretti/Salazar	333SP	1st
	Cochran	333SP	2nd
	Morgan/Evans	333SP	3rd
IMSA/WSC Watkins Glen	Moretti/Salazar	333SP	1st
IMSA/WSC Indianapolis	Moretti/Salazar	333SP	1st
	Velez/Evans	333SP	2nd
IMSA/WSC Laguna Seca	Velez/Evans	333SP	1st
	Salazar	333SP	2nd
	Dale	333SP	3rd
	Cochran	333SP	4th
1995			
Canadian GP	Jean Alesi	412T2	1st
Sebring 12 Hrs	Evans/Velez/Van de Poele	333SP	1st
IMSA/WSC Lime Rock	Wayne Taylor	333SP	1st
IMSA/WSC Texas	Wayne Taylor	333SP	1st
	Michele Alboreto	333SP	2nd
IMSA/WSC Phoenix	Fermin Velez	333SP	1st
BPR GT Anderstorp	Ferte/Thevenin	F40 LM	1st
1996			
Spanish GP	Michael Schumacher	F310	1st
Belgian GP	Michael Schumacher	F310	1st
Italian GP	Michael Schumacher	F310	1st
IMSA/WSC Road Atlanta	Moretti/Papis	333SP	1st
IMSA/WSC Lime Rock	Moretti/Papis	333SP	1st
IMSA/WSC Watkins Glen	Moretti/Papis	333SP	1st
BPR GT Anderstorp	Della Noce/Olofsson	F40GTE	1st
1997			
Monaco GP	Michael Schumacher	F310B	1st
Canadian GP	Michael Schumacher	F310B	1st
French GP	Michael Schumacher	F310B	1st
Belgian GP	Michael Schumacher	F310B	1st
Japanese GP	Michael Schumacher	F310B	1st
Sebring 12 Hrs	Dalmas/Johansson/Velez/Evans	333SP	1st

Event	Drivers	Car	Position
WSC Lime Rock	Hermann/Montermini	333SP	1st
WSC Mosport Park	Morgan/Fellows	333SP	1st
WSC Pikes Peak	Hermann/Montermini	333SP	1st
WSC Sebring	Hermann/Montermini	333SP	1st
1998			
Argentine GP	Michael Schumacher	F300	1st
Canadian GP	Michael Schumacher	F300	1st
French GP	Michael Schumacher	F300	1st
	Eddie Irvine	F300	2nd
British GP	Michael Schumacher	F300	1st
Hungarian GP	Michael Schumacher	F300	1st
Italian GP	Michael Schumacher	F300	1st
	Eddie Irvine	F300	2nd
Daytona 24 Hrs	Moretti/Theys/Luyendyk/Baldi	333SP	1st
Sebring 12 Hrs	Baldi/Moretti/Theys	333SP	1st
USRRC Las Vegas	Taylor/Van de Poele	333SP	1st
USRRC Watkins Glen	Moretti/Theys/Baldi	333SP	1st
ISRS Paul Ricard	Theys/Lienhard	333SP	1st
ISRS Brno	Sospiri/Collard	333SP	1st
ISRS Misano	Sospiri/Collard	333SP	1st
ISRS Donington Park	Sospiri/Collard	333SP	1st
	Lienhard/Theys	333SP	2nd
	Calderari/Bryner/Zadra	333SP	3rd
ISRS Anderstorp	Sospiri/Collard	333SP	1st
	Lienhard/Theys	333SP	2nd
ISRS Nurburgring	Sospiri/Collard	333SP	1st
ISRS Le Mans	Sospiri/Collard	333SP	1st
	Lienhard/Theys	333SP	2nd
Petit LM Road Atlanta	Taylor/Van de Poele/Collard	333SP	1st
1999			
Australian GP	Eddie Irvine	F399	1st
San Marino GP	Michael Schumacher	F399	1st
Monaco GP	Michael Schumacher	F399	1st
Austrian GP	Eddie Irvine	F399	2nd
German GP	Eddie Irvine	F399	1st
	Eddie Irvine	F399	1st
	Mika Salo	F399	2nd
Malaysian GP	Eddie Irvine	F399	1st
	Michael Schumacher	F399	2nd
ISRS Barcelona	Sospiri/Collard	333SP	1st
	Moncini/Pescatori	333SP	2nd
	Baldi/Redon	333SP	3rd
	Lavaggi/Mazzacane	333SP	4th
	Calderari/Bryner	333SP	5th
	Zadra/Zadra	333SP	6th
ISRS Monza	Sospiri/Collard	333SP	1st
	Baldi/Redon	333SP	2nd
	Calderari/Bryner	333SP	3rd
	Waaijenberg/Van der Lof	333SP	4th
SRWC(ISRS) Spa	Baldi/Redon	333SP	1st
	Sospiri/Collard	333SP	2nd
SRWC Enna	Moncini/Pescatori	333SP	1st
SRWC Magny Cours	Lavaggi/Mazzacane	333SP	1st
USRRC Lime Rock	Theys/Lienhard	333SP	1st

This appendix contains only major events where Ferrari scored an outright victory. Where provided, placings are given to indicate the Ferrari strength in a particular race. In addition, there are countless high placings in championship races, and numerous victories in various categories worldwide. Up to the end of 1999 Ferrari drivers had won a total of 125 World Championship grand prix races since the inauguration of the series in 1950.

* = GT Category Winner

(NC) = Non Championship

CHAMPIONSHIP VICTORIES

1952	World Drivers' Championship	Alberto Ascari
1953	World Drivers' Championship	Alberto Ascari
	World Sports Car Championship	
1954	World Sports Car Championship	
1956	World Drivers' Championship	Juan Manuel Fangio
	World Sports Car Championship	
1957	World Sports Car Championship	
	Australian Gold Star Championship	Lex Davison
1958	World Drivers' Championship	Mike Hawthorn
	World Sports Car Championship	
1960	World Sports Car Championship	
1961	World Drivers' Championship	Phil Hill
	F1 Constructors' Championship (Established in 1958)	
	World Sports Car Championship	
1962	Speed World Challenge	
	European Mountain Championship	Ludovico Scarfiotti
1963	Speed & Endurance World Challenge	
1964	World Drivers' Championship	John Surtees
	F1 Constructors' Championship	
	International Championship for Makes	
1965	International Championship for Makes	
	European Mountain Championship	Ludovico Scarfiotti
1967	International Championship for Makes	
1968	Temporada Championship (ARG)	Andrea de Adamich
1969	Tasman Cup	Chris Amon
	European Mountain Championship	Peter Schetty
1970	Tasman Cup	Graeme Lawrence
1970/71	New Zealand Gold Star Series	Graeme Lawrence
1972	World Championship for Makes	
1975	World Drivers' Championship	Niki Lauda
	F1 Constructors' Championship	
1976	F1 Constructors' Championship	
1977	World Drivers' Championship	Niki Lauda
	F1 Constructors' Championship	
1979	World Drivers' Championship	Jody Scheckter
	F1 Constructors' Championship	
1982	F1 Constructors' Championship	
1983	F1 Constructors' Championship	
1992	Italian Super Car GT Championship	Rory Parasiliti/F40
1993	Italian Super Car GT Championship	Marco Brand/F40
1994	Italian Super Car GT Championship	Vittorio Colombo/F40
1995	IMSA/WSC Manufacturers' Championship 333SP	
	IMSA/WSC Drivers' Championship	Fermin Velez
1998	ISRS Drivers' Championship	Sospiri & Collard
	ISRS Team Championship	JB-Giesse/333SP
1999	F1 Constructors' Championship	
	SRWC Drivers' Championship	Sospiri & Collard
	SRWC Team Championship	JB-Giesse/333SP

SUMMARY

Nine Drivers' Titles (Established 1951):

1952	Alberto Ascari
1953	Alberto Ascari
1956	Juan Manuel Fangio
1958	Mike Hawthorn
1961	Phil Hill
1964	John Surtees
1975	Niki Lauda
1976	Niki Lauda
1979	Jody Scheckter

Nine Constructors' Titles (Established 1958):
1961, 1964, 1975, 1976, 1977, 1979, 1982, 1983, 1999.

Twelve Manufacturers' Titles (Established 1953):
1953, 1954, 1956, 1957, 1958, 1960, 1961, 1962, 1963, 1964, 1965, 1967.

FERRARI FORMULA ONE DRIVERS

Kurt Adolff (D)
Michele Alboreto (I)
Jean Alesi (F)
Cliff Allison (GB)
Chris Amon NZ)
Mario Andretti (USA)
Rene Arnoux (F)
Alberto Ascari (I)
Giancarlo Baghetti (I)
Lorenzo Bandini (I)
Rubens Barichello (BR)
Jean Behra (F)
Derek Bell (GB)
Gerhard Berger (A)
Bob Bondurant (USA)
Tony Brooks (GB)
Ivan Capelli (I)
Piero Carini (I)
Eugenio Castellotti (I)
Johnny Claes (B)
Peter Collins (GB)
Gianfranco Comotti (I)
Andrea de Adamich (I)
Alfonso de Portago (E)
Max de Terra (CH)
Alejandro de Tomaso (RA)
Charles de Tornaco (B)
Juan Manuel Fangio (RA)
Giuseppe Farina (I)
Rudolf Fischer (CH)
Paul Frere (B)
Nanni Galli (I)
Olivier Gendebien (B)
Richie Ginther (USA)
Ignazio Giunti (I)
Jose Froilan Gonzalez (RA)
Dan Gurney (USA)
Mike Hawthorn (GB)
Phil Hill (USA)
Peter Hirt (CH)
Jacky Ickx (B)
Eddie Irvine (GB)
Stefan Johansson (S)

Chico Landi (BR)
Nicola Larini (I)
Niki Lauda (A)
Roger Laurent (B)
Umberto Maglioli (I)
Willy Mairesse (B)
Nigel Mansell (GB)
Robert Manzon (F)
Arturo Merzario (I)
Gianni Morbidelli (I)
Luigi Musso (I)
Mike Parkes (GB)
Reg Parnell (GB)
Cesare Perdisa (I)
Andre Pilette (B)
Didier Pironi (F)
Alain Prost (F)
Clay Regazzoni (CH)
Carlos Reutemann (RA)
Pedro Rodriguez (MEX)
Ricardo Rodriguez (MEX)
Louis Rosier (F)
Mika Salo (SF)
Roy Salvadori (GB)
Ludovico Scarfiotti (I)
Giorgio Scarlatti (I)
Jody Scheckter (RSA)
Harry Schell (USA)
Rudolf Schoeller (D)
Michael Schumacher (D)
Dorino Serafini (I)
Andre Simon (F)
Raymond Sommer (F)
John Surtees (GB)
Jacques Swaters (B)
Patrick Tambay (F)
Piero Taruffi (I)
Maurice Trintignant (F)
Nino Vacarella (I)
Gilles Villeneuve (CAN)
Luigi Villoresi (I)
Wolfgang Von Trips (D)
Peter Whitehead (GB)

MAJOR MODEL SPECIFICATIONS

SINGLE-SEATERS

YEAR	MODEL	ENGINE SIZE	CYL'S	BORE & STROKE	INDUCTION	BHP	GEARS
1948	125 GP	1497cc	V12/60°	55x52.5mm	SSC	230@7000rpm	5
1948	166 F2	1995cc	V12/60°	60x58.8mm	3TCC	155@7000rpm	5
1949	125 F1	1497cc	V12/60°	55x52.5mm	TSC	260@7000rpm	5
1949	166 FL	1995cc	V12/60°	60x58.8mm	SSC	310@7000rpm	5
1950	375 F1	4494cc	V12/60°	80x74.5mm	3TCC	350@7000rpm	4
1951	212 F1	2563cc	V12/60°	68x58.8mm	3TCC	200@7500rpm	5
1952	500 F2	1985cc	4 In Line	90x78mm	2TCC	200@7500rpm	4
1952	375 Indy	4494cc	V12/60°	80x74.5mm	3TCC	430@7500rpm	5
1953	553 F2 Squalo	2498cc	4 In Line	100x79.5mm	2TCC	240@7500rpm	4
1954	625 F1	498cc	4 In Line	94x90mm	2TCC	210@7000rpm	4
1955	555 F1	2498cc	4 In Line	100x79.5mm	2TCC	240@7500rpm	4
1956	D50 F1	2488cc	V8/90°	73.6x73.1mm	4TCC	260@8000rpm	5
1957	801 F1	2499cc	V8/90°	80x62mm	4TCC	275@8200rpm	5
1957	156 F2	1489cc	V6/65°	70x64.5mm	3TCC	180@9000rpm	4
1958	246 F1	2417cc	V6/65°	85x71mm	3TCC	270@8300rpm	4
1961	156 F1	1477cc	V6/65°	73x58.8mm	3TCC	185@9200rpm	5
1961	156 F1	1477cc	V6/120°	73x58.8mm	2TrCC	190@9500rpm	5
1962	156 F1	1477cc	V6/120°	73x58.8mm	2TrCC	190@9500rpm	6
1963	156 Aero F1	1477cc	V6/120°	73x58.8mm	PI	200@10200rpm	5
1964	158 F1	1489cc	V8/90°	67x52.8mm	4TCC	210@11000rpm	5
1964	1512 F1	1490cc	Flat 12	56x50.4mm	PI	220@12000rpm	5
1965	1512 F1	1490cc	Flat 12	56x50.4mm	PI	225@11500rpm	5
1966	312 F1	2990cc	V12/60°	77x53.5mm	PI	375@10000rpm	5
1967	312 F1	2990cc	V12/60°	77x53.5mm	PI	390@10000rpm	5
1967	166 F2	1596cc	V6/65°	86x45.8mm	PI	200@10000rpm	5
1968	312 F1	2990cc	V12/60°	77x53.5mm	PI	412@10500rpm	5
1968	246 Tasman	2405cc	V6/65°	90x63mm	PI	285@8900rpm	5
1969	312 F1	2990cc	V12/60°	77x53.5mm	PI	436@11000rpm	5
1970	312B F1	2991cc	Flat 12	78.5x51.5mm	PI	450@12000rpm	5
1971	312B2 F1	2991cc	Flat 12	78.5x51.5mm	PI	470@12600rpm	5
1973	312B3 F1	2992cc	Flat 12	80x49.6mm	PI	485@12500rpm	5
1975	312T F1	2992cc	Flat 12	80x49.6mm	PI	500@12200rpm	5
1976	312T2 F1	2992cc	Flat 12	80x49.6mm	PI	500@12200rpm	5
1978	312T3 F1	2992cc	Flat 12	80x49.6mm	PI	510@12200rpm	5
1979	312T4 F1	2992cc	Flat 12	80x49.6mm	PI	515@12300rpm	5
1980	312T5 F1	2992cc	Flat 12	80x49.6mm	PI	515@12300rpm	5
1981	126CK F1	1496cc	V6/120°	81x48.4mm	2TuCh	560@11500rpm	5
1982	126C2 F1	1496cc	V6/120°	81x48.4mm	2TuCh	580@11000rpm	5
1983	126C3 F1	1496cc	V6/120°	81x48.4mm	2TuCh	600@10500rpm	5
1984	126C4 F1	1496cc	V6/120°	81x48.4mm	2TuCh	660@11000rpm	5
1985	156/85 F1	1496cc	V6/120°	81x48.4mm	2TuCh	780@11000rpm	5
1986	F1-86 F1	1496cc	V6/120°	81x48.4mm	2TuCh	850@11500rpm	5
1987	F1-87 F1	1496cc	V6/90°	81x48.4mm	2TuCh	880@11500rpm	6
1988	F1-87/88C F1	1496cc	V6/90°	81x48.4mm	2TuCh	620@10000rpm	6
1989	640 F1	3498cc	V12/65°	84x52.6mm	PI	600@12500rpm	7
1990	641 F1	3498cc	V12/65°	84x52.6mm	PI	680@12750rpm	7
1991	642 F1	3499cc	V12/60°	86x50.2mm	PI	710@13800rpm	7
1992	F92A F1	3498cc	V12/65°	n.a.	PI	700+@n.a.	6
1993	F93A F1	3498cc	V12/65°	n.a.	PI	700+@n.a.	6
1994	412T1 F1	3498cc	V12/65°	n.a.	PI	700+@n.a.	6
1995	412T2 F1	2997cc	V12/75°	n.a.	PI	c.600@n.a.	6
1996	F310 F1	2998cc	V10/75°	n.a.	PI	600+@n.a.	6
1997	F310B F1	2998cc	V10/75°	n.a.	PI	650+@n.a.	7
1998	F300 F1	2997cc	V10/80°	n.a.	PI	700+@n.a.	7
1999	F399 F1	2997cc	V10/80°	n.a.	PI	750+@n.a.	7
2000	F1-2000	2997cc	V10/80°	n.a.	PI	770+@n.a.	7

INDUCTION KEY

SSC – Single-Stage Supercharger	3TCC – Three Twin-Choke Carburettors	2TrCC – Two Triple-Choke Carburettors
TSC – Two-Stage Supercharger	3FCC – Three Four-Choke Carburettors	4TrCC – Four Triple-Choke Carburettors
1TCC – One Twin-Choke Carburettor	4TCC – Four Twin-Choke Carburettors	PI – Petrol Injection
2TCC – Two Twin-Choke Carburettors	6TCC – Six Twin-Choke Carburettors	2TuCh – Twin Turbochargers

SPORTS RACING & GT CARS

YEAR	MODEL	ENGINE SIZE	CYL'S	BORE & STROKE	INDUCTION	BHP	GEARS
1947	125S	1497cc	V12/60°	55x52.5mm	3TCC	118@7000rpm	5
1948	166 SC	1903cc	V12/60°	60x58.8mm	3TCC	150@7000rpm	5
1949	166MM	1903cc	V12/60°	60x58.8mm	3TCC	140@6600rpm	5
1951	212 Inter	2563cc	V12/60°	68x58.8mm	3TCC	170@6500rpm	5
1951	340 America	4102cc	V12/60°	80x68mm	3TCC	220@6000rpm	4
1951	212 Export	2563cc	V12/60°	68x58.8mm	1TCC	150@6500rpm	5
1952	340 Mexico	4102cc	V12/60°	80x68mm	3TCC	280@6600rpm	4
1953	250MM	2953cc	V12/60°	73x58.8mm	3FCC	240@7200rpm	4
1953	340MM	4102cc	V12/60°	80x68mm	3FCC	300@6600rpm	4
1953	375MM	4522cc	V12/60°	84x68mm	3FCC	340@7000rpm	4
1953	735S	2941cc	4 In Line	102x90mm	2TCC	220@6000rpm	5
1954	250 Europa GT	2953cc	V12/60°	73x58.8mm	3TCC	220@7000rpm	4
1954	375 Plus	4954cc	V12/60°	84x74.5mm	3TCC	344@6500rpm	4
1954	500 Mondial	1985cc	4 In Line	90x78mm	2TCC	160@7000rpm	4/5
1954	750 Monza	2999cc	4 In Line	103x90mm	2TCC	260@6000rpm	5
1955	121LM	4412cc	6 In Line	102x90mm	3TCC	360@6000rpm	5
1956	250GT LWB	2953cc	V12/60°	73x58.8mm	3TCC	250@7000rpm	4
1956	290MM	3490cc	V12/60°	73x69.5mm	3FCC	320@7300rpm	4
1956	860 Monza	3432cc	4 In Line	102x105mm	2TCC	280@6000rpm	4
1956	500TR	1985cc	4 In Line	90x78mm	2TCC	190@7400rpm	4
1956	625LM	2498cc	4 In Line	94x90mm	2TCC	225@6200rpm	4
1957	315S	3783cc	V12/60°	76x69.5mm	6TCC	360@7800rpm	4
1957	335S	4023cc	V12/60°	77x72mm	6TCC	390@7800rpm	4
1957	500TRC	1985cc	4 In Line	90x78mm	2TCC	190@7400rpm	4
1958	250TR	2953cc	V12/60°	73x58.8mm	6TCC	290@7500rpm	4
1959	250TR/59	2953cc	V12/60°	73x58.8mm	6TCC	300@7200rpm	5
1960	250GT SWB	2953cc	V12/60°	73x58.8mm	3TCC	250@7400rpm	4
1962	250GTO	2953cc	V12/60°	73x58.8mm	6TCC	290@7400rpm	5
1962	196SP	1984cc	V6/60°	77x71mm	3TCC	200@7800rpm	5
1962	248SP	2458cc	V8/90°	77x66mm	4TCC	250@7500rpm	5
1962	268SP	2645cc	V8/90°	77x71mm	4TCC	260@7500rpm	5
1962	330TRI/LM	3967cc	V12/60°	77x71mm	6TCC	390@7500rpm	5
1963	330LM	3967cc	V12/60°	77x71mm	6TCC	390@7500rpm	4
1963	250P	2953cc	V12/60°	73x58.8mm	6TCC	300@7800rpm	5
1963	330P	3967cc	V12/60°	77x71mm	6TCC	370@7300rpm	5
1964	250LM	3286cc	V12/60°	77x58.8mm	6TCC	320@7500rpm	5
1964	275GTB/C	3286cc	V12/60°	77x58.8mm	6TCC	260+@7400rpm	5
1964	275P	3286cc	V12/60°	77x58.8mm	6TCC	320@7700rpm	5
1964	330P	3967cc	V12/60°	77x71mm	6TCC	370@7300rpm	5
1965	166P	1593cc	V6/65°	77x57mm	3TCC	175@9000rpm	5
1965	206P	1987cc	V6/60°	86x57mm	3TCC	205@8800rpm	5
1965	275P2	3286cc	V12/60°	77x58.8mm	6TCC	350@8500rpm	5
1965	330P2	3967cc	V12/60°	77x71mm	6TCC	410@8200rpm	5
1965	365P	4390cc	V12/60°	81x71mm	6TCC	380@7300rpm	5
1966	275GTB/C	3286cc	V12/60°	77x58.8mm	3TCC	260+@7400rpm	5
1966	206S	1987cc	V6/65°	86x57mm	PI	240@8800rpm	5
1966	330P3	3967cc	V12/60°	77x71mm	PI	420@8200rpm	5
1967	330P4	3967cc	V12/60°	77x71mm	PI	450@8200rpm	5
1967	350 Canam	4176cc	V12/60°	79x71mm	PI	480@8500rpm	5
1968	612 Canam	6222cc	V12/60°	92x78mm	PI	620@7000rpm	5
1969	212E	1991cc	Flat 12	65x50mm	PI	300@11800rpm	5
1969	312P	2990cc	V12/60°	77x53.5mm	PI	430@9800rpm	5
1969	712 Canam	c.7000cc	V12/60°	n.a.	PI	c.700@n.a.	5
1970	512S	4994cc	V12/60°	87x70mm	PI	550@8500rpm	5
1971	365GTB/4C	4390cc	V12/60°	81x71mm	6TCC	350+@7500rpm	5
1971	312PB	2991cc	Flat 12	78.5x51.5mm	PI	450@10800rpm	5
1971	512M	4994cc	V12/60°	87x70mm	PI	550@8500rpm	5
1975	365GT4/BB	4391cc	Flat 12	81x71mm	4TrCC	380+@7700rpm	5
1978	512BB/LM	4942cc	Flat 12	82x78mm	PI	480@7200rpm	5
1980	308GTB Gp4	2927cc	V8/90°	81x71mm	PI	250+@7700rpm	5
1988	F40LM	2855cc	V8/90°	80x71mm	2TuCh	500+@7000rpm	5
1993	348GT/C	3405cc	V8/90°	85x75mm	PI	320+@n.a.	5
1994	333SP	3997cc	V12/65°	n.a.	PI	600+@11000rpm	5
1996	F40GT-E	3500cc	V8/90°	n.a.	2TuCh	620+@7000rpm	6
1996	F50 GT1	4700cc	V12/65°	85x69mm	PI	550+@8500rpm	6

Index